Day by Day with God

ROOTING WOMEN'S LIVES IN THE BIBLE

SEPTEMBER–DECEMBER 2011

Christina Press
BRF
Tunbridge Wells/Abingdon

First published in Great Britain 2011

ISBN 978 1 84101 636 8

Distributed in Australia by:
Willow Connection, PO Box 288, Brookvale, NSW 2100.
Tel: 02 9948 3957; Fax: 02 9948 8153;
E-mail: info@willowconnection.com.au

Distributed in New Zealand by:
Scripture Union Wholesale, PO Box 760, Wellington
Tel: 04 385 0421; Fax: 04 384 3990;
E-mail: suwholesale@clear.net.nz

Acknowledgments

Scripture quotations taken from The Holy Bible, New International Version, copyright
© 1973, 1978, 1984, 1995 by International Bible Society. Used by permission of
Hodder & Stoughton Publishers, a member of the Hachette Livre UK Group. All rights
reserved. 'NIV' is a registered trademark of International Bible Society. UK trademark
number 1448790.

Scripture quotations taken from The Holy Bible, Today's New International Version,
copyright © 2004 by International Bible Society. Used by permission of Hodder &
Stoughton Publishers, a member of the Hachette Livre UK Group. All rights reserved.
'TNIV' is a registered trademark of International Bible Society.

Scripture quotations taken from The New Revised Standard Version of the Bible,
Anglicised Edition, copyright © 1989, 1995 by the Division of Christian Education of
the National Council of the Churches of Christ in the United States of America, are
used by permission. All rights reserved.

Scripture quotations from THE MESSAGE. Copyright © by Eugene H. Peterson 1993,
1994, 1995. Used by permission of NavPress Publishing Group.

Scripture quotations from the Holy Bible, New Living Translation, copyright © 1996,
2004. Used by permission of Tyndale House Publishers, Inc., Wheaton, Illinois 60189.
All rights reserved.

New King James Version of the Bible copyright © 1979, 1980, 1982 by Thomas
Nelson, Inc. All rights reserved.

Scripture quotations marked ESV are from The Holy Bible, English Standard Version,
published by HarperCollins Publishers © 2001 Crossways Bibles, a division of Good
News Publishers. Used by permission. All rights reserved.

Printed in Great Britain by CPI Bookmarque, Croydon

Contents

Contributors

Alie Stibbe works in Business Support in a College of Further Education. She is also a freelance writer and mother of four. She is married to Mark Stibbe, Director of The Father's House Trust: www.thefathershousetrust.com

Jennifer Rees Larcombe has six children, all married, and loves playing with her numerous grandchildren. She runs Beauty from Ashes, an organisation that helps to support people adjusting to bereavement and trauma.

Molly Dow, a retired bishop's wife, grandmother of seven, and Anglican Reader, has produced courses on prayer and spirituality, written *Mountains and Molehills* and, with her husband, co-written *When He Comes*.

Abidemi Sanusi is a writer and editor of www.readywritermag.com, an online magazine for Christians who enjoy reading and writing. Her last book, *Eyo*, was shortlisted for the 2010 Commonwealth Writers' Prize.

Lyndall Bywater lives in Canterbury with her husband, her housemate, her assorted guide dogs and a cat. She is passionate about prayer: writing about it, promoting it and training people in it.

Ali Herbert is based in central London and is a freelance writer. She also plays keyboards in the band Pastiche and runs children's music workshops. She is married to Nick and they have two children, Gracie and Josiah.

Jean Watson is a writer, a spiritual director and a director of a local counselling service. Her work has included teaching, editing and writing for different age groups and media—books, magazines, radio and TV.

Elaine Pountney coaches Christian leaders in spiritual formation and also facilitates workshops on 'Reclaiming the wonder of sexuality'. Currently she offers inspiration to a church plant on Vancouver Island, specialising in an exciting 'Parables in the pub' outreach.

Catherine Butcher has edited *Day by Day with God* since 2003. She loves using words to help Christians grow spiritually and put faith into practice. She and her husband Adrian have two teenage children and live in Sussex.

Catherine Butcher writes...

Plans for the 2012 Olympics are gathering pace. All over the world athletes are in training, preparing to travel to London for the events. Those of us who won't be taking part but were quick off the mark to apply for tickets will be looking forward to joining the crowds to cheer on the competitors.

Have you ever thought of the crowds we have cheering us on from heaven? The author of Hebrews describes a 'great cloud of witnesses' who are doing just that. Hebrews 11 describes some of the witnesses: Abraham, Isaac, Jacob, Joseph, Moses and many more. And in Hebrews 12 the writer challenges us: 'Since we are surrounded by such a great cloud of witnesses, let us throw off everything that hinders and the sin that so easily entangles, and let us run with perseverance the race marked out for us. Let us fix our eyes on Jesus, the author and perfecter of our faith, who for the joy set before him ensured the cross, scorning its shame, and sat down at the right hand of the throne of God. Consider him who endured such opposition from sinners, so that you will not grow weary and lose heart' (vv. 1–3, NIV). The chapter goes on to encourage us to accept God's discipline as training which will result in righteousness and peace.

In this set of daily readings, several contributors focus on Bible characters: many of these characters will be among that 'great cloud of witnesses'. As you take time out each day to listen to God, to read the Bible and to talk to God about your life and concerns, draw on the examples of Bible characters, but, more than anything, keep focusing on Jesus. As you look to him, invite the Holy Spirit to work in your life so that you will be changed more and more into Jesus' likeness (2 Corinthians 3:18).

Just as we don't see that great cloud of witnesses, we might not notice how we are becoming more like Jesus. When you love someone and want to please them, you change, often without realising it. It's the same in our relationship with Jesus. We are transformed by his grace as we keep our focus on him.

In this third part of the year, determine daily to focus on Jesus, thanking your heavenly Father for his love and inviting the Holy Spirit to transform you to be more like him.

Never enough

You have planted much, but have harvested little. You eat, but never have enough. You drink, but never have your fill. You put on clothes, but are not warm. You earn wages, only to put them in a purse with holes in it.

Over the next ten days I will be sharing some thoughts with you on the subject of 'contentment'. I chose this topic because I am approaching my 50th birthday and have come to a point in life where it is natural to try to figure out what life is all about and what I really want out of what is left of it—circumstances permitting!

Looking back, it seems that much of the last 15 years of my life has been spent trying to prove something to myself and the world around me. What else would motivate a woman to study for a PhD, write and translate several books and run a company, while raising four children and supporting a husband in full-time parish ministry? And I do mean all at once! Perhaps I am simply exhausted now that I have settled our family into a home of their own rather than in a vicarage, but, whatever the reason, all this 'chasing after the wind' (Ecclesiastes 2:11) does not seem to have the appeal it once had.

Despite running round in ever-decreasing circles, I have tried to keep the Lord as the focus of what I have done (Proverbs 3:6). Not so the people to whom today's passage was addressed. Their activity and acquisitiveness had led them to ignore what the Lord was calling them to do with their time and resources. I'm sure they had good harvests, warm clothes, lovely food, excellent wine and well-stitched purses, but the God-shaped hole in their souls created a situation in which they could never say that what they had was enough. In my experience, making the Lord the focus of your life changes your perspective on what is enough and changes your definition of success.

....

Delight yourself in the Lord and he will give you the desires of your heart. Commit your way to the Lord; trust in him; and he will do this: he will make your righteousness shine like the dawn (Psalm 37:4–6).

ALIE S

The Lord is my portion

I say to myself, 'The Lord is my portion; therefore I will wait for him.' The Lord is good to those whose hope is in him, to the one who seeks him; it is good to wait quietly for the salvation of the Lord.

I have a garden that is far from finished: it is quite wild in places, because I do not have as much time to spend in it as I would like. Nevertheless, as I stare over the vegetable beds in the late summer sunshine, I feel a deep sense of contentment and I am reminded that we always have a choice, even if it is only a choice of attitude. I do not think contentment is merely a state of mind; it is more than that. In Proverbs 23:7, we read '… as he thinks in his heart, so is he' (NKJV): what we believe deep down influences the kind of person we are and the way we think and behave. From this I understand that contentment must be a product of the soul, coming from within, rather than something we acquire from the trappings of life. So what is true contentment?

Some of the earliest references to the state of contentment in Jewish thought use an expression made up of two words, one meaning 'happiness' or 'joy' and the other meaning 'portion' or 'lot'. Put together, contentment can be understood as 'being happy with one's lot in life or one's portion'. This mindset is totally at odds with the kind that can never say 'Enough!' It promotes an attitude that compels us to 'want what we have' rather than 'have what we want'.

Some of us may think that our lot in life is nothing to write home about, but we should remember that 'the Lord is our portion' and that nothing about our physical circumstances can separate us from his love. Being happy that we are in relationship with God is the source of the deepest contentment a human being can experience: 'Then one rests content, untouched by trouble' (Proverbs 19:23).

....

Lord, thank you that, in you, my lot is secure, that you fill me with joy in your presence, with eternal pleasures at your right hand—and I am satisfied.

ALIE S

The satisfied soul

I will praise you as long as I live, and in your name I will lift up my hands. My soul will be satisfied as with the richest of foods; with singing lips my mouth will praise you.

If true contentment is the state of being happy or joyful with my 'lot in life' or 'portion', and if the Lord is my portion, it follows that great contentment comes from rejoicing in the Lord—in who he is and what he has done for us. I truly believe that if we intentionally culti-vate a grateful attitude towards the Lord, our sense of spiritual con-tentment will deepen as the days go by.

The psalmist in today's reading says that his soul will be satisfied as with the richest of foods. This does not mean that he is going to a physical banquet; it means that praising God feeds his soul so that he is more than satisfied to the depths of his being. In our Bibles, the two words 'contentment' and 'satisfaction' often translate the same Hebrew word. Both English words have the connotation of being 'filled up'. 'Contentment' makes us think of the 'content' of life— what it is filled with—and 'satisfaction' comes from two Latin words that mean 'to make full'. So spiritual contentment can be thought of as a state that we attain when we fill up our life with content that is focused on the Lord, primarily through praising and thanking him.

Cultivating this kind of soul attitude does not mean that we become mindless triumphalists. It is a fact of life that we have to face difficulties just like everybody else. The difference is in the way we react. Those who have the Lord as their portion are not shaken to the same degree as those who do not. Contentment is the assurance of faith that God's provision is sufficient for our needs and that God's grace is sufficient for every circumstance.

....

Lord, fill up my heart with praise and thankfulness for all that you have done for me and all you have given me through the unending sufficiency of your grace.

ALIE S

Job satisfaction

When God gives people wealth and possessions and the ability to enjoy them, to accept their lot and be happy in their work—this is a gift of God.

Although spiritual contentment is a product of the work of God's Spirit in our soul, there is no way we can separate ourselves from the fact that we live in a material universe. To live, we have to meet various physical needs. We need shelter, food and clothing, and these things are usually provided by having a job.

I have been back at work outside the home for four years, and in that time I have had jobs including cleaning, working in a delicatessen and being a personal assistant. Now I work in a college as an administrator. Often I have struggled with these jobs. I have been tempted to think I am cut out for 'better things' (whatever they are), just because I have spent so many years studying and collecting qualifications. In God's economy, though, we are called to be happy in our work and to realise that the job we have been put in, and the reward we get for our labours, is a gift from God himself. This means that there is no excuse for the kind of muttering I sometimes indulge in; instead we should work hard and strive for excellence so that we do not bring God's name into disrepute.

Does this mean, then, that we should not seek any advancement in our careers? Not necessarily. Sometimes we are called to downsize our work role, but I do not think it is wrong to seek advancement if we are not driven solely by pride and selfish ambition, but by a desire to please God and do our part in providing adequately for our dependants. If that is the case, we can trust that, in God's good time, 'the desires of the diligent [will be] fully satisfied' (Proverbs 13:4).

....

Lord, I thank you for the work that you have given me to do. Help me to fulfil my tasks diligently so that I might know your gift of authentic job satisfaction.

ALIE S

Pay day blues

Keep your lives free from the love of money and be content with what you have, because God has said, 'Never will I leave you; never will I forsake you.'

I expect I am just like many people with a salaried job: I look forward to pay day with inexplicable anticipation, even though I know that the amount typed in the bottom right-hand corner of that impossible-to-open envelope will be the same as last month's, give or take a penny or two. The amount never changes and I don't expect it will for a year or so, now that there is a freeze on public-sector spending. I rather miss working for myself, because when you have your own business there is always the possibility that, if you work harder and longer, your income might actually increase. Not so in a salaried job. When you work for someone else, the pay stays the same and the potential to become dissatisfied and grumble about your income is considerable—especially at busy times of the year when working harder does not mean more money.

Recently we had a couple of minor disasters at home, which rather focused my mind on the fact that my income never changes. How can we cater for unexpected emergencies if there is never enough to save and never the possibility that my income might improve? One thing led to another and I sat and calculated how much of a pay rise I would need to be able to pay off our mortgage in the remaining duration of my potential working lifetime. Don't ask! It was more than is humanly possible.

When we come to the end of ourselves, it is a good time to throw ourselves back into the arms of the God who has promised never to fail or forsake us. I may be looking at how I can supplement my income, but my trust in the Lord's provision has also grown in the process.

....

Lord, help me to be grateful for the income you have given me and help me to use it wisely so that I can be content with what I have.

ALIE S

Fed up?

*When you have eaten and are satisfied, praise the Lord your God
for the good land he has given you. Be careful that you do not
forget the Lord your God, failing to observe his commands, his
laws and his decrees.*

One of my favourite pastimes is picking a well-calculated moment
for my supermarket shop, in the hope that I will find some bargains
on the reduced-price produce stands. An hour too soon and you are
too early for the second price cut to 75 per cent off; a quarter of an
hour too late and everything has gone! The rewards of getting it right
can be considerable. My best coup was ten chickens at 56p each.
They went straight in the freezer and fed us Sunday lunch for almost
three months. I can still remember the look on the faces of the couple behind me in the checkout queue. The woman could not understand why I should want ten chickens. First, it had never crossed her
mind that they could be frozen for later, and, second, her partner
commented that they would rather die than buy anything from the
reduced-price counter. Well, my family and I are still alive to tell the
tale and those cheap organic chickens tasted amazing—especially
with vegetables straight from our garden. There was plenty for everyone and much praise forthcoming for the cook.

The temptation for the canny shopper, though, is to start thinking
that your good fortune is down to your own expert timing—when, in
fact, rather like the provision of quails in the desert, an abundance of
cut-price chickens, Lincolnshire sausages or sliced multigrain loaves,
and a freezer to store them in, are the contemporary version of Lord's
provision for us in an economic desert. When we have eaten and
been satisfied, it is good not to forget that the source of our culinary
contentment is God's faithfulness and goodness—whether that food
carries a yellow cut-price sticker or a top brand label.

....

*Lord, thank you for the food you give us to satisfy our hunger.
May we never forget that you are our provider, however simple or
extravagant the meal placed before us might be.*

ALIE S

What's in your backpack?

Godliness with contentment is great gain. For we brought nothing into the world, and we can take nothing out of it. But if we have food and clothing, we will be content with that.

Having written about being satisfied with the food the Lord provides, it would be tempting to move on to ask how full our wardrobes are of clothes that we never wear, while we still hanker for more. Having just watched an interesting film with a subtext about life's 'baggage', my mind was focused to realise that today's passage is not about the amount or quality of food we crave or how up-to-date or expensive our wishlist wardrobe might be, but about all the other stuff we think we have to fill our lives with in order to be content or satisfied.

A stuffed backpack is cumbersome and weighs us down. In the same way, a life full of unnecessary belongings, or the craving after more or better consumables, is unbearably heavy and slows us down. Usually we don't realise quite how much it slows us down until we have shed some of the baggage—in the same way that we don't realise how physically tired we've become until we've lost a stone or so in unnecessary weight we've been carrying around. This was brought home with a vengeance last night when one of our children got upset about the fact that an older sibling could afford—and had bought—several items of electronic gadgetry that outshone the similar items this child had. Not easy to resolve!

Today we are encouraged to understand that godliness with contentment is the greatest gain—not the latest model of laptop with all-singing, all-dancing graphics software. To have God, the all-sufficient one, living in our hearts is to begin to experience his 'all-sufficiency' on a daily basis, because 'in Christ the fullness of the Deity lives in bodily form, and [we] have been given fullness in Christ' (Colossians 2:9–10).

....

Lord, help me to fix my eyes on you, the fullness of him who fills all in all. Help me to strip off all that hinders me and holds me back, so that I might know true godliness with contentment.

ALIE S

Life's ups and downs

I have learned to be content whatever the circumstances. I know what it is to be in need, and I know what it is to have plenty. I have learned the secret of being content in any and every situation, whether well fed or hungry, whether living in plenty or in want.

The verses quoted above may be the ones we immediately remember when we think of contentment, but how many of us really know what it means to have learned this lesson? To have '*learned* the secret of being content in any and every situation' implies that extremes of circumstance have been experienced and deep spiritual lessons have consequently moulded our character. Although things can get quite tight on the financial front some months, I would not say that our family has ever known what it is like to live in persistent want—although we did once have to throw ourselves on the mercy of the diocesan almoner when our children were very young and state benefits hardly topped up a curate's stipend enough to save us from encroaching debt. Thankfully we were never made homeless, but we did learn how to say 'No'—even to necessities—and how to rejoice in small treats when they came our way.

At the other extreme, life in a wealthy parish can become so comfortable that you can forget how to depend on the Lord for your 'daily bread' and take luxuries for granted. Of the two extremes, learning to live with excess is more difficult in spiritual terms than learning to live with want. One of my favourite verses has always been the prayer in Proverbs 30:8–9: 'Give me neither poverty nor riches, but give me only my daily bread. Otherwise, I may have too much and disown you and say, "Who is the Lord?" Or I may become poor and steal, and so dishonour the name of my God.' At last I feel that our current circumstances have struck a happy balance, but it would be hard to know that without having been to the extremes.

....

'Who seeks more than he needs, hinders himself from enjoying what he has. Seek what you need and give up what you need not. For in giving up what you don't need, you'll learn what you really do need.'
SOLOMON IBN GABIROL, 11TH CENTURY

ALIE S

More than enough to spare

Honour the Lord with your wealth, with the firstfruits of all your crops; then your barns will be filled to overflowing, and your vats will brim over with new wine.

The 'grabbit' is a strange animal that visits our house on occasions. It popped up its nasty little head the other dinner time. There were four pork chops and four people at the table. The chops were not large but they were 'enough' in the sense that 100g (4oz) of meat is a healthy portion. I had cooked lots of vegetables and delicious gravy to compensate. One family member groaned, 'Those chops are so small!' I had eaten a large free lunch at work that day, so I offered my pork chop to the 'grabbit', who felt bad that I would then be without meat, and refused the offer. Once the plates were full of meat and vegetables and gravy, everyone realised they had more than enough to eat and no room for pudding.

Now the lesson here is not about the fact that I offered my pork chop because I'd had a big lunch—that would have been no sacrifice—but that our attitude and perception play a large part in what we consider to be enough to satisfy or content us. We think we need two pork chops because that's what we've always had, and so we complain when we are given one, when in fact one is enough. In our case, it was probably my fault for overfeeding the family in the past, but, that aside, if we make time to reconsider what is enough, we find that what we have is usually plenty and to spare (2 Chronicles 31:10). This kind of exercise is very useful when we think that we haven't got enough to be able to honour the Lord with our wealth— whether it be money or runner beans. The cultivation of contentment helps us realise that we have enough to give, just as giving helps us learn to cultivate contentment.

....

Lord, help me to give of what you have given me with a grateful heart, so I can find that what I have left is more than enough to satisfy my needs.

ALIE S

The bedrock of humility

Do nothing out of selfish ambition or vain conceit… Do everything without complaining or arguing, so that you may become blameless and pure, children of God without fault in a crooked and depraved generation, in which you shine like stars.

Whenever I concentrate on getting to the bottom of what it means to cultivate a particular spiritual attribute, I end up contemplating the nature of humility. Humility is the linchpin that holds so many spiritual attributes together, including contentment. In today's passage, Paul exhorts his readers to humbly consider others to be better than themselves and to have the attitude of Christ, who took the nature of a servant.

Humility must foster contentment, because no one who has true contentment can be selfishly ambitious or full of vain conceit, unreasonable or argumentative. By definition they are happy with who they are, where the Lord has placed them and what he has given them in terms of material provision. So, to cultivate contentment, we must be sure of our call to everything we do and fulfil that calling with a servant heart and the mind of Christ.

I find it helpful to think of my administrative job as a calling. After all 'administration' is a spiritual gift, is it not (1 Corinthians 12:28)? So I try to approach all the tasks I have to do with a servant heart, because I am employed primarily to make other people's roles easier. I will admit, there are days when I struggle with being at so many people's beck and call, as I'm sure you do too—whether at home or in the workplace—but, as we seek to learn contentment, let us remember that it is 'God who works in [us] to will and to act according to his good purpose' (v. 13), in whatever role we find ourselves. If we want to know the inner repose of spiritual contentment, we must allow him to mould our will and actions by his Spirit.

....

Lord, help me be content to grow where you have planted me. Help me produce the fruit of your Holy Spirit from a quiet life of humble service.

ALIE S

September brings different reactions from different people. For some, the end of the summer and the prospect of darker, colder winter days starts a downward spiral of gloom and grumbling. Others like the possibility of new beginnings and fresh starts that autumn brings: the back-to-school, new-term feeling of excitement hasn't worn off from childhood.

How about you? Whatever the weather and whatever your circumstances, are you cultivating the attitude of gratitude that Alie Stibbe has been recommending? Are you benefiting from the contentment Paul wrote about when he told Timothy, 'Godliness with contentment is great gain' (1 Timothy 6:6)?

Over the next two weeks, Jennifer Rees Larcombe will be highlighting some of the characters in the Bible and the way they reacted to the different circumstances they faced in life. Although they lived in a very different age, human nature hasn't changed through the passing millennia. We face similar fears and failures, joys and sorrows, even though many of us live in affluence matching that of royalty in biblical times. With fresh water on tap, food to eat, clothes and homes, we have so much to be grateful for.

As you take time out each day to read the Bible passages and Jen's notes, ask God to speak specifically into your life's circumstances, encouraging you, teaching you and pointing you in new directions. Ask him to give you his eyes, to see the world and people around you as he sees them. Ask for a fresh injection of his love for those you meet and Jesus' servant heart to minister to the lives of others. Invite God to cultivate the fruit of his Holy Spirit in your life and expect opportunities to bear fruit through simple acts of kindness. They might seem small to you, but they can make a world of difference to the people around you.

Snapshots

There was also a prophetess, Anna… She was very old; she had lived with her husband seven years after her marriage, and then was a widow until she was eighty-four. She never left the temple but worshipped night and day, fasting and praying.

My bedroom walls are covered with photos; I love being surrounded by the faces of the people I love. As a counsellor I spend my life looking at faces, watching for the slightest change of expression, and, because faces fascinate me, I often wonder what my favourite Bible characters looked like. Perhaps Anna had a face like Mother Teresa of Calcutta, deeply etched with lines of love and peace.

After being tragically widowed so young, Anna would have been expected to marry again; instead she wanted to commit her whole life to being with God. For her, that meant living permanently in his house and enjoying his company, but, to me, developing that kind of intimate relationship with the Lord seems to have nothing to do with buildings or locations: it's a way of life. Whether I'm out at work, caring for my grandchildren or at home alone, I'm trying to cultivate the habit of bringing him into everything I do each day, turning every job or activity into an act of worship, whether it's chopping vegetables or writing emails.

People who came to the temple for the Jewish feasts would always see Anna's radiant face there in the corner (see Psalm 34:5). Because she spent her time focusing on God, her face would have reflected his glory and compassion So visitors would have shared their worries with her for her prayers and God would have spoken his wisdom to them through her. Miss Watt was the 'Anna' in our church; also in her 80s, she lived so close to God that she glowed with his love; we would ask her to pray about all the little personal things that worried us.

....

Making God our closest companion is the greatest life-goal we can have.

To discover King David's goal, read Psalm 27:4; for Paul's, see Philippians 3:10.

JENNIFER RL

Eli

Now Eli the priest was sitting on a chair by the doorpost of the Lord's temple. In bitterness of soul Hannah wept much and prayed to the Lord.

Like Anna, Eli lived continuously in God's house (1 Samuel 3:2), but there the likeness ends! I imagine his face looking like Friar Tuck's, fat and jolly (4:18). Greed was his downfall; when people brought animals to sacrifice, he and his sons would steal the best meat for themselves (2:29). He preferred peace to conflict and was too easygoing to stop his sons from sleeping with female worshippers (2:22–24). He didn't bother to heed God's repeated warnings until it was too late.

So often, there is something in our lives that God keeps asking us to clean up, but we put off doing anything until it destroys the person God longs for us to be.

Isn't it difficult when we see a friend heading for trouble? We may feel that God wants us to warn them but we're scared of their rejection. Yet I'm so grateful to the brave friends who have spoken the truth to me because God's opinion mattered more to them than mine did.

Perhaps Eli's greatest sin was his failure to pray for his sons. When he was warned of the disaster they faced, he weakly accepted it instead of pleading with God for mercy (3:13, 18). Samuel, the child Eli brought up, must have realised this, because years later he said that failing to pray for the people who matter to us is sin (12:23). We often think of prayer as a 'nice little thing' we can do—if we remember; but if only we really believed in the enormous, dynamic power of prayer, we would realise that it is the greatest thing we can do for anyone.

....

The bad things we do to people are often more easily forgiven than the good things we fail to do.

See why Father God's opinion mattered more to Jesus than anyone else's: Matthew 10:28, 32–33.

JENNIFER RL

Mrs Phinehas

She died in childbirth, but before she passed away the midwives tried to encourage her… 'You have a baby boy!' But she did not answer or pay attention to them. She named the child Ichabod (which means 'Where is the glory?').

Poor Mrs Phinehas! I pity her, yet her story has helped me several times. She had just heard that her husband and father-in-law were dead, but that wasn't why she lost the will to live. In spite of being a priest, her husband was a womaniser, godless and evil (1 Samuel 2:12, 22). His father was blind and 98 years old (4:15), so he had had a full life. No, the worst part of the scenario for her was the loss of the ark of the covenant. This golden box was seen as a symbol of God's presence and approval, and it had been her family's responsibility to guard it. Instead, her husband had dragged it into battle, where it was captured by the Philistines. She called her baby the equivalent of 'God's gone' because she felt that he had been defeated and had abandoned her.

I've felt like that three times in my life. I was terrified because God no longer seemed in control of all the chaos and tragedy that were overwhelming me. I thought, 'Either God doesn't care or he's power-less to help and the devil has won!' Yet now, with hindsight, I can see that God was there all the time, and out of all that turmoil he has *invariably* brought enormous benefits to my entire family.

If only Mrs Phinehas had realised that Eli's death would allow Samuel to become the great leader his people lacked, ushering in the golden age under David and Solomon. She died of despair because she couldn't see God's big picture.

....

If bad things are hitting you, and God doesn't seem to be doing much about it, remember that he is waiting just round the corner with quantities of blessings to lavish on you. Trust him just a little bit longer!

JENNIFER RL

Jochebed

She became pregnant and gave birth to a son. When she saw that he was a fine child, she hid him for three months. But when she could hide him no longer, she got a papyrus basket... placed the child in it and put it among the reeds along the bank of the Nile.

When I went with my daughter for her 20-week scan, we gloated over the tiny hands and feet we could see on the screen. Then the doctors told us that the baby could not survive birth. Jochebed also knew that her baby would die—if it were a boy. Pharaoh had commanded that every boy born to his slaves must be drowned, but when Moses was born, Jochebed hid him because she believed that God would protect him (Hebrews 11:23). All the same, pushing that basket out into the river must have been the most agonising thing she ever did.

There was once someone whom I loved in such a possessive way that I tried to control her, wrapping her in cotton wool. 'You'll lose her if you don't give her freedom to be herself,' a brave friend told me. 'Hold her out to God on an open hand.' I did, and was sad when she 'flew away', but later she came back to me and we formed a new and healthier relationship.

Is there someone you need to 'push out into the river and entrust to God's care'? Rather than a person, could it be a role or ministry you built up until it became your 'baby'? Is it time to trust God to bring blessing without your involvement? If Jochebed had tried to keep Moses hidden, she would have lost him. It was only by entrusting him to God that she had him back (vv. 8–9).

As his wet-nurse, Jochebed taught Moses about the God she trusted. Although he left his own people and their God and became 'an alien in a foreign land' for many years (Exodus 2:22), Moses eventually remembered everything his mother had taught him.

....

Lord, I bring you the people
I love who have turned their
backs on you. Please restore
their faith.

If you have a 'prodigal', let Jesus' story keep your hope alive: Luke 15:11–24.

JENNIFER RL

Jonathan

Saul's son Jonathan went to David at Horesh and helped him find strength in God. 'Don't be afraid,' he said. '… You will be king over Israel, and I will be second to you.'

I think Jonathan must have had a noble face. His sheer unselfishness staggers me! He was heir to his father's throne and had every quality needed for the role. He was a man of faith (1 Samuel 14:6), a brave and powerful soldier (v. 14), a great leader (v. 7) and very wise (vv. 29–30). Yet he willingly stepped aside for David. Why? Because from the moment they met, Jonathan 'became one in spirit with David, and he loved him as himself' (18:1). So often, we love our friends because they make us feel good or perhaps because we need their help to achieve our own private goals. Sometimes, we are so terrified of being rejected by them that we let them walk all over us. Real love, however, unselfishly wants what is best for a friend.

Because they shared everything, David would definitely have told Jonathan that God had promised to make him king one day. A man with less faith than Jonathan's would have been jealous, but, because he trusted and honoured God above anything, he was totally happy to help God—and David—fulfil the promise. Isn't it difficult faithfully to support someone above us at work or in church, being consistently willing to give them the limelight by staying in the shadows ourselves, when we know we have just as many gifts and strengths as they have? Yet Jesus said, 'Anyone who wants to be first must be the very last, and the servant of all' (Mark 9:35, TNIV). He wants us all to have servant hearts. If you are called to be a leader, remember how important it is to serve others by facilitating and affirming other people's gifting.

....

Jonathan turned up exactly when David needed encouragement because his faith was wobbling and he felt scared and alone. Lord, make me that kind of a friend.

JENNIFER RL

Joshua

The Lord said to Joshua, '… Have I not commanded you? Be strong and courageous. Do not be terrified; do not be discouraged, for the Lord your God will be with you wherever you go.'

Joshua's face, as he gazed across the Jordan towards Jericho, would probably have looked rather scared! Like Jonathan, he too had a servant heart and had been quite content to be Moses' sidekick for 40 years—watching him leading a couple of million people towards their promised land. Now, suddenly, he had to take over that role himself.

For years I lived in my father's spiritual shadow. He looked like God to me! When he died, my faith plummeted dangerously for a while. Have you ever sheltered behind someone else, fed off their spiritual strength and been happy to let them take control of everything? Is God calling you to be a Joshua now and take more of a lead—at least in some area of your life?

People probably said, 'It's all down to you now, Joshua.' That could have made him feel crushed by responsibility, but God wanted Joshua to know that he would be just as much with him as he had been with Moses (v. 9). He also told Joshua the secret of staying safely surrounded by his care—meditating on God's word day and night (v. 8). The same applies to anyone who has been asked by God to do something new and challenging. Joshua experienced amazing success, perhaps because God gave him supernatural gifts for the job: 'Now Joshua son of Nun was filled with the spirit of wisdom because Moses had laid his hands on him. So the Israelites listened to him and did what the Lord had commanded' (Deuteronomy 34:9). James 1:5 says that wisdom is ours for the asking! God never asks us to do a job for him without also giving us all we need to get it done.

Lord, please change my fear of inadequacy into faith in your power.

See how Paul encouraged Timothy when handing over leadership to him: 1 Timothy 4:12–15; 2 Timothy 1:7.

JENNIFER RL

Lazarus

Jesus, once more deeply moved, came to the tomb… 'Take away the stone,' he said… Jesus called in a loud voice, 'Lazarus, come out!'

A snapshot of Lazarus, shuffling out of the tomb, bandaged like a mummy, would look terrifying! We know he shared a home with his sisters Mary and Martha; they all loved having Jesus to stay, and his sisters described Lazarus as the 'one Jesus loved' (John 11:3). Of course Jesus doesn't love some people more than others, but Lazarus and John (John 20:2) were just more *sure* of that love—which is how we all should be!

Lazarus had seen Jesus do so many miracles that, when he was taken ill himself, he must have been convinced that Jesus would rush to his bedside and heal him. As he felt his life ebbing away, did he feel as let down and angry as Mary and Martha were (11:21, 32)?

He had been dead four days and his body had been sealed inside a tomb when his spirit heard Jesus call his name. There are times in our lives when we also feel trapped in darkness, perhaps through depression, illness or major loss. Maybe we feel as if Jesus has let us down, too. It often takes a lot of courage to begin to edge our way back towards him when we hear his voice calling us into the light. We are hampered by the 'grave clothes' that still wrap us around, but we have to make that first vital decision to respond to his call before he can command us to be totally set free. Recovering from a time of spiritual 'deadness' can feel daunting, and many of us feel safer staying hidden in the darkness, but I'm sure Lazarus would tell us that the effort was worth it.

....

Lord, I know there are areas of my life that have died—my enthusiasm for serving you, belief in the power of prayer or my compassion for others. Please draw these dead parts of me back into your light.

JENNIFER RL

23

Samson

Then Samson prayed to the Lord, 'O Sovereign Lord, remember me. O God, please strengthen me just once more.'

Yesterday, as I walked past our local gym, a young man emerged, stripped to the waist to reveal his amazing muscles. As he swaggered away looking invincible, I thought, 'Samson must have looked just like that. No wonder women were his downfall!'

An angel had promised Samson's parents that he would become a great warrior—but only if he remained totally dedicated to the Lord. As a sign of his commitment, he must never touch alcohol or cut his hair (Judges 13:5). God's gift of supernatural strength made him a superhero—until he met Delilah. She was the seductive enemy spy who stole Samson's devotion to God and cracked the secret of his strength. Chained in a dark prison in Gaza, poor Samson felt as if God had abandoned him because of his failure.

Failure doesn't bother some people; they learn from it and move on. For others, it's devastating. Perhaps because of our upbringing, some of us are driven by the need to do everything perfectly. Failure in relationships, career or ministry leaves us chained in a dungeon of regret and despair. We need to remind ourselves firmly that, if it is possible always to be perfect, then Jesus died for nothing. Samson didn't have the advantage of knowing Jesus but, as his hair began to grow (16:22), his faith returned. When thousands of Philistines gathered in their temple to taunt him, Samson prayed for supernatural strength just once more—and managed to bring down the roof. He destroyed more enemies in his death than he had in a lifetime.

'Since I messed up my marriage and got into bad debt, I feel that people despise me,' said Jamie. Actually, they didn't, he just thought they did because he despised himself. Although Jamie had received God's forgiveness, he also had to forgive himself.

....

Do you need to ask God to restore your spiritual strength?

See how Jesus reacted after Peter's awful failure: John 21:15–19.

JENNIFER RL

Naomi

But Ruth replied, 'Don't urge me to leave you... Where you go
I will go, and where you stay I will stay. Your people will be my
people and your God my God.'

'Before and after' photos of Naomi would be most revealing. Setting
off to emigrate to a foreign land with her husband and two boys,
her face would have looked full of hope. Ten years later, when she
returned to Bethlehem without them, grief made her face unrecognis-
able (v. 19); but at least she wasn't alone.

Of all the various human relationships, I think being a mother-
in-law is often the trickiest. Naomi must have been an exception-
ally good one for Ruth to cling to her like that. It is often difficult
to live out our faith in our own families, but Naomi had done it so
effectively that Ruth was ready to embrace all her beliefs. Perhaps the
secret was that Naomi prayed for her daughters-in-law (v. 9).

Life was so tough for widows in those days that Naomi's faith was
tested fiercely, but, because Ruth trusted her enough to follow her
advice, God was able to lead them to the one man who could help
(2:19–20). This story has a gorgeous ending, with Naomi holding her
baby grandson while all the neighbours exclaim, 'He'll make you
young again! He'll take care of you in old age. And this daughter-
in-law who has brought him into the world and loves you so much,
why, she's worth more to you than seven sons!' (4:15, The Message).

For years I thought my mother-in-law was a dragon; and perhaps
she thought I was! We both seemed to threaten each other because
we were so different from each other. Then one day, through reading
the book of Ruth, I felt the Lord asking me to pray for an improve-
ment in our relationship. It took years before anything changed, but
when she became frail, frightened and lonely, the wall between us
finally came down.

....

*If you have a tricky relationship
with a daughter- or mother-in-
law, ask God for his healing.*

For more of this beautiful love
story, read Ruth 3.

JENNIFER RL

Zerubbabel

So [the angel] said to me, 'This is the word of the Lord to Zerubbabel: "Not by might nor by power, but by my Spirit,' says the Lord Almighty.'

Here is another strong face to add to our portrait gallery. I think of Zerubbabel every time something I have to do feels impossibly difficult. He was born in Babylon, where his nation was in exile, yet God gave him a passion to lead his people home. He spearheaded the first band of enthusiasts to reach Jerusalem, only to find that the Babylonians had left his land in heartbreaking ruins. Zerubbabel knew that God wanted them to start by rebuilding the temple, but, after a half-hearted attempt, discouragement set in (perhaps because they were working in their own strength). The people went off to build their own homes and reclaim the desecrated farmland; but 16 years later the temple was still a ruin, while crops and business ventures failed.

Zerubbabel probably asked, 'Why is life so tough, Lord?' God answered through a prophet, who told them that they were all so busy with their own families and careers, they were not giving worship first priority in their lives (see Haggai 1:6–9). Doesn't that sound horribly familiar? Once Zerubbabel and his followers had got their priorities right, God 'stirred up' their spirits (Haggai 1:14) and their enthusiasm for temple building was reignited. 'Be strong… and work' said the Lord. 'For for I am with you' (Haggai 2:4).

Some mornings, when I can't face a lengthy 'to do' list, I ask the Lord for the spiritual gifts of efficiency and enthusiasm. With those, plus extremely hard work, Zerubbabel and his team finished rebuilding the temple in an amazingly short time. God doesn't want us to burn out by working in our own strength, but our 'to do' lists won't get finished if we sit back and wait for a miracle. Partnership with God means our hard work is empowered by his supernatural strength.

....

Lord, I'm overloaded. There is no time for me—or you—in my life. Help me to cope by sharing your yoke (Matthew 11:28–30) and keeping close to you.

JENNIFER RL

Uzziah

His fame spread far and wide, for the Lord gave him marvellous help, and he became very powerful. But when he had become powerful, he also became proud, which led to his downfall.

Uzziah's face, at 16, would have looked anything but self-confident: he was too young to become king. He had godly advisers, though, who helped him transform his lack of self-confidence into God-confidence. God gifted him to the point of genius: everything he did was an astounding success. As his self-confidence grew, though, his God-confidence waned.

Pride is the most dangerous sin of all because it deceives us into thinking that we don't need God's help or forgiveness. The more intelligent and gifted we are, the more prone we are to pride; but it is also a sin to stay hiding in our inadequacy rather than allowing God to help us become the person he wants us to be.

Once Uzziah had finished reorganising the army, farming methods and town planning, he turned his attention to the temple. 'These priests are totally inefficient,' he must have thought. But the priests didn't want to be reorganised: that was God's prerogative. When Uzziah burst into the Holy of Holies, where God allowed only priests to go, he was confronted by 80 furious clerics. Uzziah was not used to opposition and he might have had all the priests executed, but suddenly he found himself covered with leprosy. At that moment, the Jewish historian Josephus tells us, an earthquake rocked Jerusalem (see Amos 1:1). Poor Uzziah was hustled away, banished from human society for ever, while his son took his crown. God doesn't often deal with pride quite so immediately, but ultimately it is an even more deadly disease than leprosy.

....

Lord, please show me any areas of my life where I have begun to trust my own abilities more than I trust you and your strength. I want you to eradicate pride from my heart—whatever that may cost. Help me to remember that everything I have comes from you.

JENNIFER RL

Hagar

[Hagar] gave this name to the Lord who spoke to her: 'You are the God who sees me.'

My imaginary portrait of Hagar has dark rebellious eyes and a wide sensual mouth. She was the slave-girl whom Abraham and Sarah used as a surrogate mother when their faith in God's promise of a son wobbled badly. Her pregnancy caused a major family row (v. 5), and perhaps Sarah and Hagar both behaved badly. Rather than trying to understand Sarah's frustrated longing for a baby, Hagar ran away in a rage; but the terrible loneliness of the desert soon defeated her. She was still angry when she had her remarkable experience of God.

The same happened to me once, when I also felt hurt, misunderstood and furious with my husband, Christian friends and God himself. I stormed out—only to fall into a pond of liquid manure. I felt as if my life was a similar mess, so I swore at God loudly; but it was then that I suddenly became aware of his presence, and his love seemed to surround me. Like Hagar, I felt that he understood how I felt and really minded for me. Once I had asked him into the centre of all my distress, he began to change the way I felt about my situation. It was the knowledge that God loved and valued us personally that gave Hagar and me the courage to go back and face our difficult situations.

It's so easy to forget our special God-encounters—but I did and so did Hagar. When she and her son caused another family row 14 years later, she found herself lost in the desert once again (Genesis 21:15–21). She forgot how God had previously met and helped her and she gave in to resentment and self-pity. Fortunately her son prayed and God not only rescued them both but also, through them, founded the entire Arab world.

....

Lord, I love those mountain-top experiences when you feel so close, but please forgive me for doubting you again so quickly when I'm down in the next valley.

JENNIFER RL

The slave girl

Naaman was commander of the army of the king of Aram…but he had leprosy. Now bands from Aram had gone out and had taken captive a young girl from Israel, and she served Naaman's wife. She said to her mistress, 'If only my master would see the prophet who is in Samaria! He would cure him of his leprosy.'

Recently I watched a TV programme about human trafficking. I'm still haunted by the faces of those women, kidnapped into appalling slavery. The girl in today's story was also snatched from her home to become a slave in a foreign land, but there was no bitterness in her determined little face. When our lives are wrecked, anger is a normal human emotion, and she probably shed many furious tears at first, but she didn't hold on to her anger until it turned to hatred. She actually wanted the best for her master.

I admire the way she kept her belief in God, even in a culture where he wasn't respected. Many of us, if we live and work with people who don't share our faith, know how easy it can be to let it go, but this young girl also had the courage to share her faith. On her recommendation, Naaman took a long journey into enemy territory to ask a favour of a king he'd already defeated. Just imagine her fate if Naaman had come home humiliated and not healed! She might have been beaten to death—while merely being laughed at stops some of us from sharing our faith in God's supernatural power to intervene in human lives. What an example she is to us all! Her story has a lovely ending, with Naaman coming home not only well again but firmly believing in her God (v. 15). Probably the whole household soon shared that young girl's faith.

....

Lord, I want my life to count like this girl's did; I long to see others turn to you because of my witness. Please give me her kind of love and courage.

For the story of another servant-girl who believed in answered prayer, read Acts 12:5, 9–16.

JENNIFER RL

The prophet's apprentice

Elisha prayed, 'O Lord, open his eyes so he may see.' Then the Lord opened the servant's eyes, and he looked and saw the hills full of horses and chariots of fire all around Elisha.

He had not been in the job long, so I guess a photo of this young lad's face might have shown him looking rather puzzled. He had always longed to become a prophet himself one day, so to be apprenticed to Elisha was the chance of a lifetime, but he soon felt discouraged and frustrated when he realised that his master operated in a dimension he simply could not understand. Elisha saw things that were invisible to others and heard God speaking to him directly.

I think a lot of us feel slightly threatened by other people's gifting. Left-brained people, who are ruled by their heads, like to be able to understand everything rationally. They can have enormous faith, but embracing the supernatural element of Christianity is harder for them than for right-brainers, who follow their feelings and intuitions and are more comfortable with the paranormal. God made us all different because he likes us that way, so we do need to accept each other just the way we are. Paul's list of the more practical spiritual gifts in Romans 12:6–8 is just as important as his list in 1 Corinthians 12:8–10.

Yet this story does seem to show that whatever personality type we have, we can all ask God for a clearer view of the spiritual world, should he want us to see it. All around us are heavenly beings, posted there to look after us (Hebrews 1:14). There are dark spirits watching us, too, but Jesus has given us his authority over them so we have nothing to fear (Ephesians 6:11–13).

....

Lord, please help me to see life from your angle and make me more aware of the 'miracle dimension'. Please give me the spiritual gift that you need me to have, to serve you best in the situations where you have placed me.

JENNIFER RL

The good, the bad and the ugly: they are all there among the characters Jen has brought to our attention over the past two weeks. Have you recognised some of your contemporaries or your own circumstances in the lives of these Bible characters? Take some time to review what God has been saying to you over the past month. Have you noticed how God has blessed you and cared for you, even in the difficult times of your life? Spend some time thanking him. Have you become aware of attitudes or aspects of your life that need to change? John says, 'If we confess our sins, he is faithful and just and will forgive us our sins' (1 John 1:9, TNIV). Are there people or situations that need your prayers? 'The prayer of a righteous person is powerful and effective,' says James 5:16.

Over the next two weeks, Molly Dow will be focusing on Paul's letters to Timothy. These practical letters are as valid for today's church as they were 2000 years ago. Paul was writing to a young leader. Some of what he wrote will be specifically applicable to your own life; other aspects might prompt you to pray for leaders in your church or denomination.

Pray especially for Christian teachers, youth leaders and leaders in uniformed organisations. They often have a thankless task. They work with young people who are changing rapidly and challenging boundaries. They can have a profound influence over a couple of years; then the young people they've worked with are off to college and the leaders have to start again, building new relationships with a fresh group. Teachers are under immense pressure and the energy and intensity of youth work can be draining. Is there any way God could use you to encourage people in your area who are working with young people?

As you consider what Paul tells Timothy about training, thank God for those who have taught and encouraged you on your journey as a Christian.

Spiritual companionship

To Timothy, my loyal child in the faith: Grace, mercy, and peace from
God the Father and Christ Jesus our Lord... I urge you... to remain
in Ephesus so that you may instruct certain people not to teach any
different doctrine... But the aim of such instruction is love.

Paul's two letters to Timothy, along with his letter to Titus, are often
called the pastoral epistles (which means 'letters'), because they are
addressed to individuals who have pastoral oversight of churches.
They are concerned with leadership, especially in matters of teaching and Christian living. This will have been important for Timothy, as
some in his church were being affected by Gnostic teachings, which
were sidetracking them into unfounded theories, speculations and
myths, as well as immorality. Paul's concern is both for Timothy to be
a good leader and for the church in Ephesus to stay true to God.

When we are young in our Christian faith, we need leaders and
older Christians to nurture and establish us in our faith. I was for-
tunate to grow up in a well-taught church and, from student days
onwards, to have had Christian friends with whom I learned much
about how to understand and live out the gospel.

In some ways we never outgrow this need: it is helpful to have
such people around us when we are older, too, especially if we, like
Timothy, are taking on positions of leadership in the church. We need
people slightly outside our immediate circle who are willing to ask us
penetrating questions about our leadership and about our Christian
lives. We need them to remind us of right priorities and principles
and to share the wisdom of their experience. These letters to Timothy
are from a wise, mature Christian leader to a younger, less experienced one. We should not be too proud to receive such help and,
when our turn comes, we should be available for younger leaders or
Christians who may look to us for help.

....

*From whom are you receiving this kind of 'spiritual companionship'?
If others are looking to you for it, how ready are you to give it?*
MOLLY D

Amazing grace

I am grateful to Christ Jesus our Lord, who has strengthened me, because he... appointed me to his service, even though I was formerly a blasphemer, a persecutor, and a man of violence. But I received mercy... and the grace of our Lord overflowed for me.

I remember a time, some years ago, when I realised that I did not feel particularly grateful to God. This did not seem good, so I prayed that I would feel more grateful to him. Soon I became increasingly aware of my sins and my sinfulness—not sins that might make you raise your hands in horror, but little selfish choices in everyday life. I felt bad about them, but I kept coming to God for forgiveness and I rediscovered the wonder of God's never-failing welcome and love for me—his amazing grace. I felt immensely grateful.

It was because Paul regarded himself as the foremost of sinners (v. 15) that he felt so grateful to God. He knew that he had not deserved to be rescued by Jesus on the Damascus road and that he had not earnt his calling to be appointed to God's service. These were gifts of God's mercy and love, so he was grateful for them.

When we think about God's grace at work in our own lives, we may think of it primarily in connection with our coming to faith at the beginning. But we do well also to recognise our need of grace throughout our Christian journey. We never cease to be sinners, so we need his mercy continually. We also need to remember that all our blessings are gifts of his grace: we never deserve or earn them. This includes the answers to our prayers, as well as the responsibilities, positions and privileges we have in the church and in life in general, which are to be used for the benefit of others. We need God's grace to continue as faithful followers of Christ throughout our lives—and not everyone manages it (v. 19).

....

For what are you most grateful to God today? How about praying for an increasing awareness of his love and grace day by day?

MOLLY D

First things first

I urge that supplications, prayers, intercessions, and thanksgivings should be made for everyone... God our Saviour... desires everyone to be saved and to come to the knowledge of the truth... I desire, then, that in every place the men should pray, lifting up holy hands without anger or argument; also that the women should dress themselves modestly and decently.

Decades ago, my mother told me about a local council meeting where they spent hours arguing about whether or not to spend £2000 on a swimming pool. Then came a decision on something that would cost about £20,000: they simply voted it through on the nod, because it was late, they were tired and many of them wanted to go home. They should have made sure they attended to the biggest items first.

If you were Paul, what might be the first thing you would urge Timothy to do in Ephesus, where people within the church were leading others astray with false teaching? Mature Christians, like Paul, will have learnt how to discern God's wisdom, and their experience of leading churches into growth can help them to tackle difficult situations. So Paul advises Timothy about his priorities and reminds him of God's ultimate aim—that everyone should be saved and understand the truth. He also urges that both men and women behave in ways that commend the gospel and do not cause unnecessary offence. These are the highest priorities at the moment. Much of the rest of his letter fleshes out in more detail what this will mean in practice.

The last few verses of chapter 2 are about what women should and should not do in church. This is too big and thorny a subject to deal with satisfactorily in these notes. What Paul says here is probably affected by the context of Ephesus at that time, when both Jews and Greeks would have been scandalised by the freedom of women to think, to learn and to teach.

....

God wants everyone to find life and well-being in and through him. Are there any ways in which you or your church have lost sight of God's priorities?

MOLLY D

Church leadership

Now a bishop [or overseer] must be above reproach… He must not be a recent convert, or he may be puffed up with conceit… Deacons likewise must be serious… And let them first be tested… Women [women deacons or deacons' wives] likewise must be serious.

Appointing or electing leaders in the church can be a difficult task. It is not always easy to discern someone's maturity, spirituality and wisdom, let alone their potential and their ability to grow into the role. Mistakes have sometimes been made—but there are qualities and actions, some of which Paul lists here, that can rule a person out of a leadership role.

Those who teach or lead the church should be able to lead it in the ways God wants. They must, therefore, know God and his ways and be living them out in their own lives, in an obedient and disciplined way. They should preach what is true and practise what they preach. To know God and his ways deeply takes time, and there is the danger that people may fall into pride, which is why Paul says that a 'bishop' should not be a recent convert. A mature Christian is less likely to think they deserve their role and more likely to know their continual need of God's mercy and grace.

Because leaders represent the church in the eyes of the world, they should not give cause for criticism or scandal in their character or behaviour; otherwise the church and the gospel of Jesus may fall into disrepute. Of course, some people may reject the gospel anyway, but let it not be for this reason. We all represent the church among our friends, family, colleagues and acquaintances, so the qualities that should be seen in our leaders need to be seen in us all.

Let us pray regularly for our leaders, who, like us, are all fallible, sinful human beings, in constant need of God's grace; furthermore, they may be under particular spiritual attack because of their role.

....

Should leaders be better than others or merely good examples of what we are all growing into?

MOLLY D

A godly balance

Everything created by God is good, and nothing is to be rejected, provided it is received with thanksgiving; for it is sanctified by God's word and by prayer... Train yourself in godliness.

I do not like watching the narrow beam exercise in women's gymnastics on television, because I am afraid of how painful it will be if the gymnast falls on to the beam. I have tried walking on a much lower bar in a playground, not very successfully, though some of my grandchildren manage it very well. What is required is good balance, which is not one of my strengths and becomes even less so as I get older.

The Gnostic heretics in Ephesus believed that spirit was good and matter, including the body, was evil. Two opposite errors followed from this belief: some said that people could do as they liked because the body would ultimately be destroyed anyway; others said that all the body's instincts should be suppressed by strict rules. For Timothy, leading the church in this context must have felt rather like walking on a narrow beam, trying to avoid both errors. Paul reminds him of the truth that matter is not evil, but good, because it is created by God. The basic bodily needs are, therefore, also good. So Christians are free to meet these needs, provided that it is with thanksgiving and prayerful obedience to God and his commandments.

To some extent, we all face a similar balancing act today, especially when the ethos of our society is not Christian. We need to find a right balance between freedom and a self-discipline that does not fall into rules and legalism. For example, we are free to eat any food but are not to be greedy; sex is good but only within marriage. Timothy is urged to train himself in godliness, so that he teaches what is right, not only in words but also by example (v. 12).

....

How can we train ourselves in godliness? Take five minutes each day simply listening to God; add in three extra acts of kindness daily; ask a mature Christian for further ideas.

MOLLY D

Love one another: our duty and joy

Do not speak harshly to an older man, but speak to him as to a father… Honour widows who are really widows… Let the church not be burdened, so that it can assist those who are real widows.

My mother-in-law became increasingly hard of hearing as she got older. When people had to keep repeating things, she sometimes quoted Leviticus 19:14: 'Curse not the deaf.' This was in fun, of course, since no one ever came even close to cursing her! Intrigued, I looked up the verse and discovered that these words are followed by '… and put not a stumbling block before the blind'. I realised that the verse was about not taking advantage of a person's misfortunes, because a deaf person would not hear a curse and a blind person would not see a stumbling block.

Paul is going even further here as he speaks about the positive duty of all Christians to care for one another, especially those who are older or suffering misfortune. First, he mentions the way to speak to one another. He is talking primarily about words of rebuke to an older man, but what he says applies more widely. He says that it should not be done harshly, but kindly, to soften the blow. We should, of course, always try to speak graciously and kindly to people.

When addressing care for widows, Paul stresses the responsibilities of everyone, including the widows themselves. There was no welfare state or social security then, so relatives were obliged to provide for their own family members in need. Paul hoped that younger widows would remarry and raise a family. Recognising that resources are finite, he did not want the church to be burdened by supporting people who could be supported in other ways, so that it could assist those in real need (v. 16). The widows themselves had the responsibility not to live lives of selfish idleness and gossip, but to give themselves to prayer and doing things for others (vv. 4–6, 10–12).

....

Paul is trying to help Timothy to lead well by building the church into a caring family. How can we do this in our own churches?

MOLLY D

Treating each other fairly

Let the elders who rule well be considered worthy of double honour, especially those who labour in preaching and teaching... Never accept any accusation against an elder except on the evidence of two or three witnesses... Do not ordain anyone hastily, and... keep yourself pure.

When I was in my first teaching job, I would sometimes go home in tears, partly because of the attitudes and behaviour of some of the pupils towards me and partly out of frustration at my own inability to control them and interest them in what I wanted to teach them. I realised later that they were not acting out of personal animosity against me, but more out of rebellion against authority figures in general, plus the desire to 'have a laugh' and impress one another. I took it personally and felt hurt, but that was not my pupils' intention.

Respect, not only for teachers but also for clergy and other ministers, has declined over recent decades. It seems that Paul, too, knew of some churches where the leaders were not well respected or even rewarded sufficiently. I have seen and heard a lot about stress and hurt among clergy, sometimes because of the way their congregations treat them. Sometimes, like me in my first teaching job, the fault is partly their own, but it is important for all of us church members to remember that our leaders are people too, with feelings. Of course they need to be able to take knocks and criticism—that goes with the job—but they are not unhurt by such attacks, especially when they are unfair, untrue or unjustified. Paul has written about wanting Timothy and the other elders to care for the church members, but he also wants the church to deal fairly with its elders (vv. 17–21).

Paul's instruction about witnesses is important: unsubstantiated gossip, or an accusation from one person who may have a grudge, should not be a basis for discipline.

....

How well do we treat the leaders (and each other) in our own church? Why do you think Paul tells Timothy not to ordain anyone hastily?

MOLLY D

Godliness with contentment

Of course, there is great gain in godliness combined with contentment; for we brought nothing into the world, so that we can take nothing out of it; but if we have food and clothing, we will be content with these.

I sometimes spend time looking at advertisements to see what they are appealing to in order to persuade us to buy their products. It seems to me that much of the advertising industry works on the basis of trying to make us discontented in various ways, then offering their products as the solution to our discontent.

We don't hear many people talking about contentment nowadays. In fact, the ethos of our society in Britain is rather the opposite. Our aim is to gain as much as possible, and, when we don't, we are prone to complain and to blame. Paul mentions people who even view their religion as being only, or primarily, about gain for themselves, which easily gives rise to envy and wrangling. He also offers us a far better alternative—godliness with contentment, which turns out itself to be great gain of a deeper and more lasting kind. The basis for it lies in an eternal perspective for those in Christ. Our money and possessions will not matter when we leave this life for heaven.

In a society where so many people are striving for more and better or seem to think they have a right to an ever-increasing standard of living, I find the thought of godliness with contentment very attractive. It implies a sense of peace that many people do not possess.

How may we discover more of this godliness with contentment? I have three suggestions: first, keep the phrase 'godliness with contentment' in your mind; second, keep working on godliness (see the note for 29 September); third, give thanks often—thank God genuinely for at least five things every day. When you can't manage all of these three, concentrate on the one you find hardest.

....

What do you think will matter most to you on your deathbed. How should this affect your life and attitudes now?

MOLLY D

The good fight of faith

But as for you, man of God, shun all [kinds of evil]; pursue righteousness, godliness, faith, love, endurance, gentleness. Fight the good fight of the faith; take hold of the eternal life, to which you were called.

Part of my work as a Spirituality Adviser was to help individuals to find a spiritual director (or spiritual companion or whatever they wanted to call it). Many of them would tell me that they wanted 'someone who will challenge me'. Whenever I needed to find a new spiritual director myself, I wanted that, too—someone who would both affirm where I was getting things right and challenge me about the areas I needed to change, to grow into all that God wanted me to be and to do. That is the kind of thing that Paul is doing for Timothy in the letter as a whole and in this passage particularly.

I am struck by the verbs Paul uses in his advice to Timothy. They are very directive: shun, pursue, fight, take hold, keep the commandment, guard and avoid. Paul's relationship with Timothy was obviously a close one: they had worked and travelled together over quite a long time and Paul uses some affectionate language in his letters. That may have been important for Timothy in receiving such directive advice from Paul. It is within a committed, safe relationship that challenges can most easily be heard, welcomed and followed.

To be a follower of Jesus will entail challenges for all of us. There is a fight of faith 'out there' as we seek to establish God's kingdom in the world, as well as 'in here', in our personal struggles with sin and temptation. We don't do anyone any favours if we present the gospel as something that makes all problems disappear. What matters is the way we face the challenges and learn through them.

At our baptism, many of us will have been prayed for to be 'Christ's faithful soldier and servant to the end of our lives'.

....

Who are the people in God's family who support and challenge you in fighting the good fight of faith?

MOLLY D

Keep on keeping on

To Timothy, my beloved child… I am reminded of your sincere faith,
a faith that lived first in your grandmother Lois and your mother
Eunice and now, I am sure, lives in you. For this reason I remind
you to rekindle the gift of God that is within you.

Paul's and Timothy's journeys into faith were very different: Timothy
came from a Christian home, whereas Paul came to Christian faith
through his dramatic Damascus road experience. My husband and
I came to faith via very different routes, too—he on a particular day
and I over a period of years. I once heard Cardinal Basil Hume say
that, after a while, how and why you began becomes less important;
it is how and why you continue now that matters.

Paul and Timothy were of rather different temperaments, too.
Once Paul had become a Christian, he put all his energy first into
learning about Jesus—what he had done and the implications of his
activities—then into taking his message to as many people and places
as possible, unafraid of the conflict that followed. Timothy, though,
seems to have been more reserved and cautious; perhaps he was a bit
afraid of conflict. Had Timothy stepped back from leadership for fear
of unpopularity or criticism? Was he finding it hard? Was he despised
for his youth (1 Timothy 4:12)? Possibly, but we don't know for certain. Paul encourages him here to keep going and not to hold back,
but to rekindle his God-given gift of leadership. He reminds Timothy
that he has God's grace (v. 9) and God's Spirit (vv. 7, 14), which is not
a spirit of fear, but of power, love and self-discipline.

Paul, now nearing the end of his life and ministry, tells Timothy of
his own experience of confidence in God's ability to keep him safe
right to the end. In effect he is saying, 'I have suffered and still suffer
for the gospel, but I am sure it has been, and still is, well worth it.
God has enabled me to keep going, so you keep on keeping on, too.'

....

*What do you find hardest about keeping going in your Christian life
and service? Do you know what would help you and where to find
that help?*

MOLLY D

Single-mindedness

Share in suffering like a good soldier of Christ Jesus. No one serving in the army gets entangled in everyday affairs... And in the case of an athlete, no one is crowned without competing according to the rules... All who cleanse themselves of the things I have mentioned will become special utensils.

You can't dabble in being a soldier: when you sign up, you know it has to be a long-term, whole-hearted commitment. The same is true for serious athletes: they need determination and self-discipline, both in their diet and in their training. Olympic athletes, especially, have to be single-minded to have a chance of winning a medal.

When we lived next to a farm, I discovered how hard farmers have to work if they are to make a living, working very long hours in all weathers, with little holiday time. To be a good soldier, athlete or farmer requires long-term commitment. It involves saying 'no' to other things, but those who go into these pursuits are willing face the cost because, for them, it is worth it. Paul is reminding Timothy that being a Christian is rather like that, too. It is a long-term commitment that involves some cost and self-discipline.

Some years ago, I went through a difficult time, which was very painful emotionally. I wondered why God allowed it. Then, one day, I sensed God asking me, 'Do you like what I am doing in you?' and I realised that he was using the difficult time to develop qualities in me that I did like. I was reminded of this when reading verses 20 and 21, about the different utensils being cleaned and shaped for their particular role in God's purposes.

We are all special utensils, each with a different use, needing to be shaped and cleaned ready for God's use. Not all formative experiences are painful, like the knocks and bumps of life, but it is those, rather than the gifts and blessings, that we tend to have trouble with.

....

Are there ways in which you need to 'clear out the clutter' that distracts you away from God's call and purpose for your life and ministry?

MOLLY D

Keeping going in tough times

In the last days distressing times will come. For people will be lovers of themselves, lovers of money... lovers of pleasure rather than lovers of God... All who want to live a godly life in Christ Jesus will be persecuted... But as for you, continue in what you have learned and firmly believed.

Perhaps it is merely that I am getting older, but it seems to be harder to be a Christian in today's world than when I was young. There is an increasingly aggressive secularism and discrimination against Christian faith in Britain. The description in verses 2–7 sounds all too familiar: the distressing end times outlined here have lasted longer than Paul anticipated. We may be tempted to think that this means the power of the gospel is failing, but, according to Paul, we should not be surprised. Distressing times are part of evil's last-ditch stand.

Yet I was particularly struck by the phrase 'people will be lovers of themselves' (v. 2), because love of self cannot be completely wrong. After all, Jesus told us to love our neighbours 'as ourselves'. Perhaps Paul is thinking of a self-love that is to the exclusion of loving God and other people. Perhaps, also, there are better and worse ways of loving oneself. Bernard of Clairvaux wrote of a 'ladder' of loves for the believer: loving self for self's sake, loving God for self's sake, loving God for God's sake and loving self for God's sake. I think this 'ladder' is well worth pondering, remembering that we may have a foot on more than one rung at a time. In our evangelism and our teaching, also, we must be careful not to foster a self-centred Christianity.

Paul gives two ways of preparing for and enduring in tough times. One is to keep reading and learning from scripture. Verses 16–17 tell us of at least four ways in which the scriptures can help us. The other way, by implication, is to be a 'lover of God' (v. 4)—the opposite of where society is going wrong.

....

In what ways do you find it hardest to love God when people around you are ignoring him or speaking against your faith? What sustains you at such times?

MOLLY D

Remember this

In view of his appearing and his kingdom, I solemnly urge you: proclaim the message; be persistent whether the time is favourable or unfavourable; convince, rebuke and encourage, with the utmost patience in teaching.

Often, at the end of a retreat, I have been encouraged to pick out two or three things that I want to be sure to remember, to write them down and make a note to review them in six months' time. I always find this irksome, but it has been useful, nonetheless. It is quite a useful exercise after a course of study, too. Also, I have heard speakers at the end of a talk say something like, 'Even if you forget everything else I have said, make sure you remember this…'.

Paul is doing a similar thing at the end of this letter. The first thing he picks out for Timothy is the high priority of going on proclaiming the message about Jesus at all times and continually helping people to apply it to their own lives, even when it is difficult and requires particular courage, patience and effort. Paul wants Timothy to remember this. The other thing Paul wants him to remember is the importance of living out the message of the gospel in his own life, both because it is right and as a good example to others. This is urgent and important because Jesus will come again, perhaps soon, so we never know how much time we have.

As he looks back, perhaps realising that he is nearing the end of his life and ministry, Paul shares something of how he feels: he has a sense of completion and of having been faithful to what God called him to do. No doubt, he hopes that his testimony will inspire Timothy to continue to fulfil his calling to teach and pass on the good news accurately and faithfully and thus, in due course, to be able to have a similar sense of completion.

....

Where are your opportunities to proclaim the message through Christ-like character and behaviour? If you are a leader, how do these verses challenge you?

MOLLY D

Personal messages

Do your best to come to me soon... When you come, bring the cloak I left with Carpus at Troas, also the books, and above all the parchments... Greet Prisca and Aquila.

Paul's personal messages are not easy to apply to ourselves, so I am going to give some personal reflections on these letters as a whole.

Paul often comes across as an intense and driven person, yet there are other sides to him that are warmer and more sensitive. I see those qualities in these final messages in his letters to Timothy, which are very human and practical. We can see that Paul cares a lot for Timothy, not only wanting to see him but also addressing him with affection. Because he cares about Timothy, he takes a lot of trouble to encourage and support him, as well as challenging him about his life and ministry. We can usefully learn to do the same for one another and to receive what others give to us in this way.

Throughout these letters, Paul stresses the importance of proclaiming the Christian message accurately, both by giving right teaching and by applying it with good examples of godly living. He wrote to a situation in which the religious ethos, even inside the church to some extent, was about playing around with a variety of ideas and speculative theories, and this made it hard for people to be sure of what was true about God and the gospel. Today, our situation is not so different. We, too, need good, clear teaching about what God has revealed to us through Jesus and through the scriptures. We need, therefore, to pray for the leaders of our churches, that they may show the love and character of God in their teaching and in their lives.

Lastly, I have been particularly struck by Paul's references to godliness: 'train yourself in godliness' (1 Timothy 4:7) and 'there is great gain in godliness combined with contentment' (6:6). I shall go on pondering these verses and trying to respond to them.

....

What has stood out for you from these letters? What difference will they make in your life?

MOLLY D

Paul's letter to Timothy is deliberately practical. His aim is to encourage this younger man to flourish and make the most of his gifts and abilities. Looking back over your life, who have been the people who have encouraged you? Have you had someone to spur you on, to encourage you through life's difficult times and to challenge you when you slip? A gifted school teacher? A loving relative? A close friend or colleague? Having someone who encourages you can make a world of difference. Even children with the most disadvantaged backgrounds can thrive and succeed with the right encouragement and mentoring.

In the Catholic tradition, a spiritual director can provide this encouragement; other traditions might refer to a discipler or mentor. Often a new Christian, a young person or someone with a particular calling or vocation is encouraged to seek out a spiritual director or mentor. We all hope that our relationship with Jesus will be such that we can learn from him—but we can all benefit from a Christian friend who will walk with us and encourage us on our spiritual pilgrimage.

Over the next two weeks, Abidemi Sanusi will be considering what it means to be daring in our faith. As you reflect on what you've learned from Paul's letter to Timothy, perhaps you need to dare to ask someone to be your spiritual coach—or perhaps you can see people around you who need encouragement in their faith. Maybe God is calling you to be a spiritual parent to some of the younger Christians in your congregation, meeting with them to pray and read the Bible together regularly, asking God to speak into the situations they face in life.

Do you dare to ask God to use you more? Be specific, calling to mind each of the people whose path crosses yours: neighbours, colleagues, friends, relatives, fellow churchgoers. How is God calling you to encourage others?

Being daring

For you did not receive a spirit that makes you a slave again to fear, but you received the Spirit of adoption. And by him we cry, 'Abba, Father.'

The *Oxford English Dictionary* defines daring as 'adventurous or audaciously bold'. The definition conjures up images of fearless people doing exciting, adventurous things. It doesn't seem to allow any space for 'normal' people such as you and me, who lead rather ordinary lives consisting of work, family and church activities, to be daring in our own right. Where in those three arenas of ordinary life are boldness and daring feats required? Nowhere, it would seem!

Being daring has different connotations for different people, though. The dictionary definition speaks of a person's ability. It reckons without the knowledge of God and his ability to work through us.

As a writer and speaker, I have the pleasure of meeting women from different countries and cultures. Conversations about our faith almost inevitably lead to comments about just how little we seem to be doing 'for God' compared with other people—and yet, when we probe further, the 'little' usually turns out to be a whole lot more daring than we previously thought.

Today's reading is a well-known one, extolling God's nature as our Father and the loving relationship we have with him. It is intended to comfort us, because it reveals the Father-heart of God. Because of this knowledge and understanding, we can rest easy, knowing that his expectations of us are based on the fact that he sees the end from the beginning—so we need not fear when we step into the unknown. Over the next two weeks, we will examine the lives of some biblical characters and explore the different ways in which they were daring in their faith and the lives they led. You may be surprised at just how much you have in common with them!

....

Dear Lord, I commit the next two weeks to you and ask you to open my heart to what you have to say to me in the area of being daring. Amen

ABIDEMI S

The visionary

Joseph had a dream, and when he told it to his brothers, they hated him all the more.

When I was a child I loved to write; later, when I became a Christian, I thought the most creative way to communicate the gospel was by writing fiction. I was not unaware of the challenging road to publication but, at the same time, I was convinced that God had called me to write, so I wrote.

Joseph was the elder of the two sons of Rachel, Jacob's beloved wife. Indeed, as one of his father's favourite sons, it could be said that Joseph led a charmed life. The Bible says, 'Now Israel loved Joseph more than any of his other sons, because he had been born to him in his old age; and he made a richly ornamented robe for him' (v. 3). When Joseph started having dreams about sheaves of corn and stars bowing down to him, he would not have been unaware of the significance of those dreams, which he foolishly recounted to his brothers.

As it turned out, Joseph was sold by his brothers to some Arab traders, who in turn sold him to one of Pharaoh's officers. For the next 15 years, his life was a tale of false accusations and imprisonment, before he was finally made prime minister of Egypt.

Whenever I read Joseph's story, I am amused by the different ways God reveals his will for our lives, ways that we do not always fully understand. I wonder, what is the big dream that you believe God has placed on your heart? Have the challenges of life taken away your ability to dream? Well, don't let them. Dare to dream again. Start with small faith-filled steps and watch where God will take you. I'm sure that Joseph never imagined he would one day be Pharaoh's second-in-command.

....

What steps are you taking to fulfil God's calling on your life?

Read Jeremiah 29:11. What do you think that verse is saying to you about your life and your dreams now?

ABIDEMI S

The reluctant leader

Moses said to the Lord, 'O Lord, I have never been eloquent, neither in the past nor since you have spoken to your servant. I am slow of speech and tongue.'

I had dinner with a fellow writer a few nights ago. We talked about the realities of the writing business—publicity interviews, speaking engagements, seminars and all the promotional activities that we do to sell our books. They are also activities that would send some shy writers running for the hills.

When I talk to novice writers about these realities, they usually say something like, 'Oh, I don't think I can do that.' The truth is that I set out to be a writer and only a writer; however, the publishing industry is such that I've had to learn to do all those promotional activities, in order to create an effective and efficient writing business.

Moses had a stutter, which, understandably, made him feel inadequate about his public speaking skills. At the same time, he was clearly a man who stood up for others, as he proved by his murder of the Egyptian who was beating up a Hebrew man. In fear of his life after committing this crime, Moses fled to Midian, where he came to the rescue of some Midianite women who were being bullied by shepherds (see Exodus 2:11–17). So, he had his strengths (righteous anger and a passion for defending the less able) and his weakness (his stutter, which gave him a fear of speaking in public).

Further readings will show that Moses remained intrinsically human: he made mistakes, but he turned them into learning experiences. Being daring is not a once-and-for-all decision; it's an ongoing journey. God is not looking for perfect followers, just people who are willing to go along with him on the faith journey. The initial step is often the most frightening one, but, just as God reassured Moses in the beginning and throughout his life, he will do the same for you.

....

Have you ever felt that God could not use you because you lacked a particular skill or personality attribute? Take the opportunity to start all over again, and lean on his ability to equip you for the task he wants you to do.

ABIDEMI S

The odd one out

[Joshua and Caleb said] 'Only do not rebel against the Lord. And do not be afraid of the people of the land, because we will swallow them up. Their protection is gone, but the Lord is with us. Do not be afraid of them.'

History is littered with people who dared to speak up against popular opinion. Yet nobody really likes being the odd one out, as it means standing out and, sometimes, being ostracised.

Joshua and Caleb were two of the twelve men who were sent into Canaan to spy out the land. I wonder what it was like for them, towards the end of their adventure, constantly reassuring the ten other men of God's promise to give Israel the land of Canaan. It couldn't have been easy: their indefatigable faith in God must have seemed annoying to the other ten men, who probably thought they were just being practical about Israel's chances of taking Canaan in battle.

That is what being daring is all about: sometimes it means being the 'difficult' one. Being difficult does not necessarily mean being unpleasant, though. It just means not bowing to popular opinion. I'm certain that all twelve spies set off for Canaan full of faith. I'm sure they sang songs testifying to God's faithfulness when they saw the riches of the land—the mountains, the sea and the fertile soil that had produced the fruits they took back to the wilderness. But then, after seeing the first Anak giant, their confidence might have been dented. It might have taken a series of events for them to start believing what their eyes were telling them about their inability to conquer Canaan.

In many ways, we are not so different. At work, perhaps there is a situation you know you should definitely challenge, but you don't want to because you don't want to stand out. This, though, is what being daring is all about—challenging the status quo and remembering those words in today's reading: 'Do not be afraid of them.'

....

Think about situations in your life that require you to speak out, and list the possible consequences. Then pray: 'Lord, I thank you that you have not given me a spirit of fear, but of power, love and a sound mind. Thank you for giving me the courage to stand out and speak up.'
ABIDEMI S

A daring wisdom

[Abigail] fell at [David's] feet and said: 'My lord, let the blame be on me alone. Please let your servant speak to you; hear what your servant has to say.'

A few weeks ago, I found myself in a situation that I just couldn't make head or tail of. As I pondered the issue, the thought came to me that I could either keep going over and over it and drive myself mad or I could quite simply pray about it and ask the Holy Spirit for help. I received a quick answer to my prayer—and it wasn't a 'spiritual' one, just a very practical way to resolve the situation.

Abigail, the woman depicted in this story, was a practical person. David and his band of men were on the run from Saul, surviving by plundering and pillaging their enemies' lands. They sent a message to Nabal, a wealthy man in Maon who had 3000 sheep and 1000 goats (v. 2), asking him to host them, in return for not hurting his sheep when they were being sheared in Carmel. Nabal was not impressed; he sent David's messengers back empty-handed. His ire raised, David vowed that not one male member of Nabal's house would be left alive by the time he and his men had dealt with him.

In the meantime, one of Nabal's servants had notified Abigail of what had happened. Abigail did a quick assessment of the situation and 'took two hundred loaves of bread, two skins of wine, five dressed sheep, five seahs of roasted grain, a hundred cakes of raisins and two hundred cakes of pressed figs, and loaded them on donkeys' (v. 18). She then sent them as a gift to David, to appease him.

Abigail was as quick-thinking as she was daring in her actions: after all, she was a married woman living in a traditional society and she was effectively going against her husband's will by giving food to David's army.

....

Lord, grant me the wisdom to act with as much spiritual and practical wisdom as necessary in all situations. Amen

ABIDEMI S

The practicalities of being daring

I set out during the night with a few men. I had not told anyone what my God had put in my heart to do for Jerusalem. There were no mounts with me except the one I was riding on.

Nehemiah was the king's wine taster. He heard news about the broken wall of Jerusalem and its burnt gates. He was very grieved about it and took it to the Lord in prayer and fasting (1:4). This shows us that Nehemiah was a man who prayed before speaking. Months later, the opportunity he'd prayed for presented itself. As he was serving King Artaxerxes, the king noticed his glum face. This in itself was punishable by death, for, as a slave, he was supposed to smile in the king's presence. Swallowing his fear, however, he prayed inwardly (v. 4) and then told the king of his desire to fix Jerusalem's wall and gates. King Artaxerxes listened and granted his wish.

Being daring also means being practical. Nehemiah did his research. He assessed the damage to the wall at night and did not tell anyone what he was doing. It was only after he had finished his assessment that he gathered the officials and told them the real reason he had come to Jerusalem.

Stepping out and doing something radical can also mean doing things within the proper institutional and legal structures. Nehemiah's plan to rebuild Jerusalem's wall was daring, but he prayed and fasted before acting. Next, he waited for an opportune moment to present his request before the king, and, even then, he prayed some more. Then he asked for official letters from the king to validate his visit to Jerusalem and also for certain governors to provide the materials he needed to get the job done.

I wonder, what ambitious and daring plans have you got in your heart? Are you so heavenly-minded that you haven't done the necessary homework for your ambitious plan?

....

Lord, I put my daring plan before you. Like Nehemiah, I pray that you will grant me favour to meet all legislative, institutional and other necessary obligations needed to make my plan work. Amen

ABIDEMI S

Making a stand

Now the king was attracted to Esther more than to any of the other women, and she won his favour and approval more than any of the other virgins. So he set a royal crown on her head and made her queen instead of Vashti.

Esther's story, as revealed in this chapter, is perplexing at first glance. She, along with many other young women (the Bible does not say how many) were prepared for a year for a night of passion with the king. If he was happy with their performance, he sent for them again, and, if he was not, they remained in the harem for the rest of their lives, unable to go back to their families. In essence, if they did not please the king, they would be imprisoned in the harem.

In light of this knowledge, what hope for Esther? She was a young Jewish girl who did not tell anyone in the palace about her Jewish background. Admitting it would surely have led to death. Yet there she was, being prepared for her night of passion with the king. We might ask, 'Where is God in the midst of such sexual sin?'

As it turned out, God gave her a friend in the eunuch Hegai. He took to Esther and prepared her in such a way that, when it came to her turn, Esther surpassed the king's expectations and was crowned the queen of Persia. Even in the midst of darkness, God can turn the most extraordinary circumstances around. Esther found herself in a situation she didn't want, yet she still lived out her faith. She was not to know that God had seen in advance what Haman (the king's adviser) planned to do, which was to destroy the Jews, and had installed her as the queen of Persia to avert this genocide.

Does Esther's story resonate with you? Do you, like Esther, find yourself in a situation not of your making, wondering where God is in it all? Then hold on: make a daring stand through your faith by living it out quietly, and watch as God turns things around.

....

Lord, I thank you that even though this situation is not of my making, you will work it out for your glory. Amen

ABIDEMI S

Living radically in the workplace

Finally these men said, 'We will never find any basis for charges against this man Daniel unless it has something to do with the law of his God.'

Many years ago, an employment agency called me. There was a job available at a company that manufactured cigarettes. Was I interested? An acquaintance once wanted to know if it is right for a Christian to work for an organisation that promotes the work of a lottery company. At first glance, some of us might think the answers are plain to see. However, if we dig a little deeper, we realise that those questions and the issues they raise are highly complex and not so different from the issues Daniel faced

Daniel was one of three governors who were responsible for a large geo-political zone in Babylon. He reported to the king. In spiritual terms, Babylon is seen as a dark, evil place. Daniel was aware of the culture and tradition of the people he was working with, yet he chose to apply himself to his work among them. It was a mark of his professional diligence that his enemies could not find accusations to raise against him, except something related to his faith.

Daniel was radical. He chose to live a life of faith in a society that was known for excess and debauchery, and that faith was reflected in his work. I am reminded of the story of a woman who worked in a bar to fund her college education. She talked about the conflict that she constantly faced as a barmaid—her faith versus her need to earn money—but then she also talked about how she helped the alcoholics in the bar, by praying for them and providing a listening ear to those who needed someone to talk to.

Our jobs may take us where we do not want to go, but, like Daniel, we can choose to live out our faith daringly, by being diligent and having a great work ethic.

....

Lord, help me to live a radical life for you in my workplace. In Jesus' name I pray. Amen

Read Matthew 5:16. In what ways do you think you can apply this verse to your own life?

ABIDEMI S

Daring to believe

Jesus said, 'I tell you the truth, this poor widow has put more into the treasury than all the others. They all gave out of their wealth; but she, out of her poverty, put in everything—all she had to live on.'

The last few years have seen a shaking in the global economy. At a personal level, it seems to have affected practically everyone I know in one way or another.

The poor widow's story is probably one of the most famous in the Bible. It is also one that will sit uncomfortably with some people in these economically challenging times. It certainly does with me. Dare I, a freelance writer, give the Lord my last two 'mites'? In asking myself this question, another one inevitably arises: do I want to?

The truth is that, as a freelancer, I have no choice but to trust God for my daily bread. In the last few years, the publishing industry has taken a battering in much the same way as the financial world. Publishers are not so keen to hand out book contracts and, with the indomitable rise of digital publishing, questions abound that continue to challenge the traditional publishing model and, consequently, authors' incomes. I ask myself again: would I really want to give God my last two mites in such financially precarious times?

After much soul-searching, I decided to go back to school last year. I barely had the funds to pay for the course, and, even as I type, the government has announced their intention to increase tuition fees threefold. I have often asked myself if I was wrong to persist in doing the course, but still I march on, in faith, committing my finances and everything else to God, because this is the path I have set myself and this is what I will do. Christianity dares us to believe in God for all our needs—because he is our Father and he cares for us. Dare you trust God with your last two mites and his promise to provide for your needs, according to his riches in glory?

....

Lord, I thank you that heaven is your throne and earth your footstool. They are all yours. You know my needs, and today I commit my finances to you, because it is all yours anyway. Amen

ABIDEMI S

Dare you be uncomfortable?

The woman said to him, 'Sir, give me this water so that I won't get thirsty and have to keep coming here to draw water.'

The enmity between the Samaritans and the Jewish people was legendary, as the latter believed that they practised true Judaism, not the mixed bag that the Samaritans practised. The woman at the well was acutely aware of the conflict (v. 20); even so, she dared to step outside her comfort zone to believe in Jesus, a Jew. Jesus himself broke cultural boundaries by speaking with her: he was a single man associating with an unknown divorced woman in a public place.

Sometimes, when I look back at my life, it would appear that I have been breaking boundaries and stepping outside my comfort zone for a long time—even if I did not always realise it. A friend told me the gospel and I responded to the call. Two years ago, I reached a crossroads in my Christian faith. For reasons too complicated to explain here, I had to leave the church I was in. I took a leap of faith and embraced another denomination. It was daunting but liberating: I have never once regretted it.

The unknown and the unfamiliar can seem frightening. Changing denominations may not seem like a big deal, but, to me, it was a very big deal. Your daring act could be something to do with moving house, to a new neighbourhood or even a new town. Perhaps you know God is calling you to do it, but you are scared: you do not know what lies there. It may be that God wants to bless you in this new place, but he can't because you're holding on to your current property and the memories that are tied up in it. If this is you, remember, God has good things in store for you, so let go and let God!

....

Father God, I thank you because I know that I can do all things through Christ who strengthens me.

ABIDEMI S

Counting the cost

Then Mary said, 'Behold the maidservant of the Lord! Let it be to me according to your word.' And the angel departed from her.

Sometimes being daring means counting the cost. Mary was a teenage girl. She knew that the price for being pregnant outside marriage was death by stoning. Her words, 'Let it be to me according to your word', show that she was prepared to face the consequences.

All over the world, Christians are counting the cost of following Christ. They are persecuted for their beliefs and, like Mary, have set their hearts and minds to follow Christ, no matter what the cost. Like Mary, they have said, 'Let it be to me according to your word.' For Christians living in the West, counting the cost means daring to live a Christ-centred life in an increasingly secular society that seems intent on marginalising Christianity through anti-Christian laws.

The Christian faith demands that the good news about Christ's salvation should be heard and shared. We are to proclaim it to everyone, regardless of whether or not they will listen. In an attempt to stem the tide of secularism, a brave woman has set up a legal centre that fights for the rights of Christians in the UK. It is a hard task and, on the face on it, an almost impossible one, but the woman and her team are not deterred. They have counted the cost: they will keep on proclaiming Christ and standing up for the rights of Christians in this country.

I ask you, when was the last time you were so daring for your faith that you had to count the cost? You may not have to, but organisations such as this legal centre run on limited funds. So dare to put your money where your faith is, by supporting organisations that campaign for religious rights all over the world.

....

I thank you that you have not given me a spirit of fear but of power, love and understanding, which enables me to count the cost of following you and yet rejoice in you. Amen

ABIDEMI S

Daring gifts for the daring Christian

Now about spiritual gifts, brothers and sisters, I do not want you to be ignorant.

Now we come to the 'one' who binds everything together: the Holy Spirit. We've spent several days thinking about the various ways we can be daring, but the truth is that the Christian life is not one that we can live in our own strength. That is why we have been given the Holy Spirit, and his gifts are there to help us live life in all its fullness, including a lot of adventures and daring faith.

As a new Christian, the first time I read 1 Corinthians 12, my prayer went something like this: 'Lord, your word says that I should desire these gifts, and I do want them, so please give them to me!' I spent the next few weeks praying meditatively—a lot of Bible reading, with worship music playing in the background, and a lot of listening. A pastor had told me that the best way to hear from the Holy Spirit was by listening: 'It might take a while but you will hear the still, small voice of the Holy Spirit.' One night, I went to a prayer meeting. A missionary was going back to her home country and we gathered round to pray for her. When I finished praying, she said, 'You really know how to hear from God. Everything you said was spot on.'

Today, many years later, I'm still listening and still learning to use the gifts listed in today's reading. I understand people's hesitancy about spiritual gifts—perhaps you've had a bad experience that has put you off—but on a personal level I know how much the development of these gifts has helped my spiritual and practical life. I pray that you too will experience these gifts and take your Christian life to a whole new level of faith.

....

Have you ever thought about asking God for spiritual gifts? Perhaps now is the time to ask, so that you can live a radically different and exciting Christian life.

ABIDEMI S

The virtues of being daring

Therefore, brethren, be even more diligent to make your calling and election sure, for if you do these things you will never stumble.

Today's reading lists several key qualities that we need if we are to live even more successful and daring Christian lives for God.

One of the qualities listed is 'virtue' (v. 5, translated 'goodness' in NIV). Having virtue means operating to Christ's standards in our work, in our homes and in everything that we do. 'Brotherly kindness' nd 'love' are mentioned as well. These could be translated as love for our feelow believers and for the people around us as we seek to live effective and productive lives that draw on God's power.

Other key qualities listed include knowledge, self-control, perseverance and godliness—all the things we need to sustain a lifetime's journey of faith. Just look at the people God called to do daring feats: David was anointed as king when he was a teenager, but he did not become king until he was in his 30s; Joseph had a dream when he was a teenager but it took about 15–20 years for the dream to come to fruition; God gave Canaan to the Israelites, but they still had to go out and take it in battle from the people who lived there. Without learning those key qualities listed above, it is doubtful whether these Bible 'greats' would ever have achieved their daring feats.

I want to focus for a moment on 'godliness'. I thank God that this is not something we are expected to achieve by ourselves, for we would never get there. It comes to us through our redeemer, Jesus. Godliness does not mean living like a doormat. No! I haven't come across any examples of godly people in the Bible who were doormats: just think of Abraham, Paul, Deborah, Sarah and Abigail.

When you live and make decisions based on the virtues listed in today's reading, you will grow in every area of your life—probably not in the way that you planned but in other, more surprising ways.

....

Lord, I thank you that I do not have to grow these qualities in my own strength, because you have given me the Holy Spirit to help me. Amen

ABIDEMI S

Bringing it all together

But I have calmed and quieted myself, I am like a weaned child with its mother; like a weaned child I am content.

In the last two weeks, we have examined different situations in which we might be daring in our faith. Some of those situations call for sacrifice and others require reflection. In light of this, it seems appropriate to end our study with something that takes us right back to basics: our father–daughter relationship with God.

Today's reading is one of my favourite psalms. It is a reminder that, for all our daring talk, our place is with God. Yes, we can be daring. Yes, we should aim to grow spiritually. Yes, we should be fearless and go out and do great things for God. In the end, though, all these things mean nothing if we do not remember where they all come from—God, who is love.

I love the simplicity of today's psalm. It only has three verses but they pack an emotional and spiritual punch. The quiet and confident declaration that the author is like a grown child who has retained his childlike trust in God never fails to bring a smile to my face.

The last verse, exhorting us to trust in God, is a great one—because, in all of our doing and daring, it can be easy to lose sight of the most important thing, which is the father–daughter relationship we have with God.

So today, as you go about your daily business, doing daring things for God, remember the psalmist's exhortation: 'O Israel, hope in the Lord. From this time forth and for ever' (v. 3, NKJV).

....

In what ways have you taken your life in your own hands and not realised that it is God's?

ABIDEMI S

In Edinburgh, the 'Try Praying' initiative (www.trypraying.co.uk) has been challenging people to give prayer a go for seven days, recording the answers to their prayers. It is a project that has prompted people who never go near a church, to ask questions about God. The team behind the initiative point to research which shows that 20 million adults in the UK pray; 13 million pray at least once a month and nine million every day. One in three people believe that God will answer their prayers.

How has God been speaking to you over the past two weeks? Are there areas of your life where you need to take new steps of faith—to be daring in new ways? All of us, probably, could dare to believe more of what we read in the Bible, to believe that God hears and answers our prayers—even if we simply took to heart the first few verses of Ephesians! What would the church be like if we truly believed that, in Christ, we are blessed 'with every spiritual blessing', that we were chosen to be holy and blameless, that we have access to his 'incomparably great power'? The anxiety, fear and guilt that limit so many of us would be gone.

Over the next two weeks, Lyndall Bywater will be focusing our thoughts on what the Bible has to say about prayer. She writes: 'I used to wonder whether I would grow out of my youthful fervour for intercessory prayer: those heady days when I believed everything was possible if we just asked God for it. Many years and hundreds of unanswered prayers later, I sincerely hope I never do.'

Whatever our circumstances or state of health, we can all be prayer warriors, daring to believe that God's promises are true and that the God who acted in power in the Bible is the same prayer-answering, powerful God today. Use the next two weeks to build spiritual muscles as you learn more about how to pray.

Mary

The angel went to [Mary] and said, 'Greetings, you who are highly favoured! The Lord is with you.'

My second guide dog was a poor judge of ponds. Unusually for a Labrador, he hated water, so ponds were something to be avoided at all costs. If the pond in question was a pleasantly sparkling expanse of clear water, he would know to steer well clear, but if it had green stuff growing on its surface, looking deceptively like grass, he would innocently stroll out on to the surface of the water without a second thought. He did not share Jesus' ability to walk on water, so his adventure would always end in a nasty algae-covered soaking.

If you want to be someone who listens to God, then you need to be ready for surprises. They may not all prove as unpleasant as Hugo's dips in ponds, but they can certainly be just as shocking, as Mary discovered when she found an angel in her living-room.

Our tendency, as human beings, is to shrink God down to a manageable size. His tendency, as almighty and everlasting God, is to remind us that he is unshrinkable. To be a person of prayer is to allow God regularly to transgress our boundaries and explode our expectations. He will not be shrunk or boxed in.

Yet, just as God will not let us limit him, nor will he let us limit ourselves. Scripture is littered with stories in which God starts conversations with people by telling them something surprising about themselves. Gideon must have been surprised to be told he was a 'mighty warrior' (Judges 6:12), and Mary was certainly surprised to hear that she was highly favoured. God's first words to us often tell us that not only is he not who we think he is, but we are not who we think we are, either.

Are you ready to be surprised today?

....

God of the unexpected, I thank you that you don't fit easily into my understanding. I invite you today to confound my expectations of you and to change my perceptions of myself. I long to see myself the way you see me, so please surprise me today. Amen

LYNDALL B

Solomon

That night God appeared to Solomon and said to him, 'Ask for whatever you want me to give you.'

A saleswoman was invited to make a presentation to the leaders of a multi-million-dollar company. She stoked up her best sales smile and stepped to the front of the boardroom. As her presentation progressed, she became more and more disheartened by the lack of engagement among her listeners. They were slumped and slouching in their seats, looking as though they were doing their best to catch up on several hours of lost sleep.

Only one man gave her any reassurance. Perched on the very edge of his seat, he was leaning towards her, looking alert and even a little enthusiastic. Afterwards she tracked him down, thinking he might be a likely sale.

'Thank you for taking such an interest in my presentation,' she said politely. 'You were really on the edge of your seat there!'

'Oh yes,' he replied. 'That's because the back of my chair was broken.'

Posture says a lot about how we listen, and, in today's reading, Solomon discovers that God's listening posture is very definitely alert, eager and perched on the edge of his seat. God doesn't wait for Solomon to bring his shopping list of kingly requests. He jumps in right from the start, asking what the king would most like in life.

As we seek to learn about prayer, the first lesson we are generally taught is that prayer isn't a slot machine—a means by which we input our wants and needs and heaven dispenses the answers at the push of a button. Prayer is a two-way relationship and a worthy end in itself, even if we never get anything back. But let us never forget the simple and heart-warming truth that God does want to hear our requests—so much so that he is on the edge of his seat, waiting for yours today.

....

Generous and compassionate Father, thank you that your ear is turned towards me. Not only do you hear me, but you listen to me. As I bring my needs to you today, teach me to walk in the joy-giving truth that you are an attentive, purposeful God. Amen

LYNDALL B

Daniel

Three times a day [Daniel] got down on his knees and prayed, giving thanks to his God, just as he had done before.

The human body has a remarkable memory. If it carries out exactly the same physical action enough times, it will simply 'remember' how to do it without needing any help from the logical mind or senses. Think about driving, for instance, or eating or knitting. How many of the actions involved in those activities does your body carry out automatically, without you really thinking about it? We are designed so that the functions most essential to our lives become more and more automatic. That way, our conscious brainpower can be reserved for the more complex tasks that we need to accomplish.

When I read this familiar old story of Daniel, I wonder if he was applying the same lessons to his soul. To choose to pray to the God of Israel when such activities were prohibited by law was a commendable thing to do, but Daniel didn't seem to be looking for accolades. He seemed to be trying to develop a 'soul memory'. He would go to the same place, kneel in the same position, face the same direction and probably say the same prayers, day after day after day.

Why would such a 'soul memory' be important? To Daniel, I suspect that it was a matter of life and death—not physical life and death (although choosing to pray like this did put his physical life in danger), but spiritual life and death. He was becoming immersed in a pagan culture that promoted the opposite of everything he believed. Perhaps he could feel his soul slipping. Perhaps this rhythm of prayer was his way of anchoring himself in God.

Much like Daniel's, the culture we live in is antithetical to prayer, so it would serve us well to develop a 'soul memory' that keeps us daily anchored into the restorer of our souls.

....

What are your rhythms of prayer? Do you have moments during the day when you automatically turn your soul towards God, no matter what you're doing? We are always in his presence, but it is good to develop habits in prayer, so that we don't drift.

LYNDALL B

Nehemiah

Those who carried materials did their work with one hand and held a weapon in the other, and each of the builders wore his sword at his side as he worked.

I had nearly fallen asleep in house group. A shameful confession, I know, but the day had been long and the sofa was comfortable. We were watching a DVD on how to live out our Christian faith in the workplace and, from the depths of my near-slumber, I was suddenly caught by a startling phrase: 'I am a warrior for God on the checkout!'

Wide awake now, I listened carefully to this enthusiastic woman and her unusual understanding of her job. She was employed at her local supermarket and took the opportunity, while serving her customers, to pray for them—hence the multitasking as warrior and checkout operative. I was impressed by her integrated approach to work and prayer, and it reminded me somewhat of Nehemiah.

Nehemiah was a man of prayer. Most of his story concerns his remarkable project to rebuild the fallen walls of Jerusalem, but that project itself was born in a prayer time. What's more, having found his inspiration in prayer, he continued to weave it through every aspect of the work. It's all too easy to become 'dualistic' in our Christian faith—to think that prayer is for our quiet time in the morning, whereas work is the 'secular' part of our lives. Nehemiah made no such separation. He didn't start out with a prayer time, asking God to bless his plans, then step into the workplace leaving God behind. He knew that he would only be able to complete his God-given calling if his work life and prayer life were inextricably linked.

Whatever your work entails today, why not make a conscious choice to hold your tools in one hand and your sword in the other? As you accomplish each task, use your God-given weapons of prayer and scripture to bless the people around you.

....

Write one of your favourite Bible verses on a piece of paper and put it somewhere you will see it while you are working. Each time you see it, let it prompt you to pray.

LYNDALL B

Hezekiah

Hezekiah received the letter from the messengers and read it. Then he went up to the temple of the Lord and spread it out before the Lord.

No matter how many years I continue in prayer, I never seem to lose a certain squeamishness about praying in a public place. Some years ago, I was on a plane on the way back from the Czech Republic, accompanied by members of a prayer team I had just been leading. All was progressing well and comfortably until the food trolley came around, and an enthusiastic member of my team suddenly leaned over and asked if he could pray for the air stewardess who was serving the food. She seemed a little fazed, but accepted nonetheless. The team member in question happens to possess an impressively resonant voice, so, as he began to pray fervently for the woman, our entire section of the plane lapsed into silence to listen. I was nearly under my seat by the time the 'Amen' came.

I wonder if it ever occurred to Hezekiah that people might think he looked a bit silly, taking his letter to the temple and spreading it out, as if for God to read. I hope it didn't. There is something wonderfully innocent and straightforward about this story of a king who is under very serious threat indeed, but immediately places himself and his people in God's hands.

When a difficulty arises, we so often resort first to problem-solving strategies, especially if we are working alongside other people. It's as though the idea of praying first is too simplistic or too embarrassing, so we have discussions and try solutions, and only when nothing has worked might we perhaps tentatively suggest praying or asking others to pray. For many of us working in secular or multi-faith environments, we can't imagine ever having the nerve to suggest prayer, even as a last resort. Yet, for Hezekiah, making prayer the first resort opened the way to an impossibly mighty victory.

....

How can you move prayer up the agenda today? Even if you can't suggest that your colleagues pray, can you make space for prayer as a first resort rather than a last?

LYNDALL B

Peter

As the men were leaving Jesus, Peter said to him, 'Master, it is good for us to be here. Let us put up three shelters—one for you, one for Moses and one for Elijah.' (He did not know what he was saying.)

'Speak' is an organisation that devotes itself to giving a voice to the voiceless, championing various causes for justice, and their recent tenth birthday celebration included some innovative and creative elements. One of these was a life-sized cardboard cut-out of a military tank. During the evening, while they were worshipping, praying and listening to the stories of the past ten years, the birthday guests were invited to cover the tank with all kinds of symbols and images of peace. By the end of the evening, the tank was transformed into a thing of beauty instead of a reminder of war.

There are many ways in which these people could have prayed for peace. They could have spoken words, they could have sung songs or they could have prayed silently in their hearts, but instead they chose to express their prayer by making something. This practical approach to prayer appears to be nothing new, judging by today's reading.

Peter was party to a prayer meeting that had gone wild. He had been asleep for the first bit (that had apparently become something of a habit for him and the two disciples with him, John and James). Then suddenly the sky lit up, a cloud came down and there before his very eyes were the two great heroes of the faith, Moses and Elijah. Prayer had suddenly gone multisensory, and now Peter was fully engaged.

What he chose to say next is fascinating. No flowery words to honour the dignity of the occasion; no falling prostrate for hours. No, for Peter the correct response to the presence and power of God was to make something—in this case, shelters.

Prayer doesn't have to be in words, or even groans or silence. Prayer can be a card sent in compassion or a cake baked in love.

....

How many of your prayers can you turn into gifts and actions today?
                                                                    LYNDALL B

Deborah

My heart is with Israel's princes, with the willing volunteers among the people. Praise the Lord!

Today we celebrate the Sues of this world. Sue was a member of our church who died almost four years ago. She never preached a sermon, led a prayer meeting or did any kind of 'public' ministry in all the time I knew her, but there was seldom a church event where she wasn't in the kitchen making coffee, and there was rarely a prayer meeting that she didn't attend. Sue was a helper and our church was so much the better for her presence.

Deborah is known for many things, not least her wisdom and her leadership skills, but as I read her story again, I find myself struck by something else about her. The generals of the army wanted her to lead them—to be their Godly figurehead—but she never wanted to assume that position. All she wanted to do was to stand alongside the 'princes' and the 'willing volunteers' among her people and help them to victory.

What always struck me about Sue was that she considered prayer as vital as service. She didn't believe in being 'too busy doing' to come to the prayer meeting. The same could be said of Deborah. When we first encounter her in Judges 4, she isn't running around being busy, managing affairs of state or leading troops into battle. She is sitting under a tree; and, given that the tree in question bears her own name, we can assume she sat there often. She was in God's presence, available and waiting for whatever or whomever he wanted to send her.

Our prayer lives are indeed about deepening our own relationship with God, but they are also our tree-times. They are the moments when we make ourselves available, so that he can send to us those who most need our help and support.

....

As you sit under your tree today, ask God who he is sending you, and how you should help them. He has prepared good works in advance for you to do (Ephesians 2:10).

LYNDALL B

Friends

Since they could not get him to Jesus because of the crowd, they made an opening in the roof above Jesus and, after digging through it, lowered the mat the paralysed man was lying on.

Using a sledgehammer is good for the soul! No set of Bible notes would be complete, for me, without lessons from the building site that is our house. When I read today's reading I find myself lost in nostalgia for the joys of swinging a large lump of lead with destructive intent. It's the stress-buster to end all stress-busters.

Sometimes prayer feels like the sledgehammer (although our intent is not usually destructive). We wield a prayer or two and walls fall down before us. Blockages are removed and breakthrough becomes reality. Some objects, though, are beyond even a sledgehammer. The iron bath, for instance, left by the previous owners, required attention from almost every tool in the house before it succumbed to being broken up. So it is with prayer. Sometimes it feels as if we've tried every prayer 50 times over and there's still not a chink of light to be seen.

The roofs of first-century houses were not easy to break through, not even with a sledgehammer. The roof was often the garden of the house, layered with building materials, waterproofing and even soil and plants. When we read that the friends made a hole in the roof, it wasn't just a matter of lifting a few tiles. They would have invested a huge amount of time and energy in digging their way through. Their compassion for their friend must have been immense.

When we talk about 'bringing our loved ones to Jesus', it sounds so easy. Yet, for many, it is a long, hard, gruelling journey of praying day after day, seeing little change but pressing on nonetheless. So today we celebrate the roof-breakers. If you have prayed the same prayer 100 times, take courage and pray it again. One day the hole will appear!

....

Pick a task that reflects your prayers: swing a sledgehammer, scrub a floor or undo a tight knot—anything that expresses in action what you're praying in your heart. As you do it, let your action become the prayer for your loved ones.

LYNDALL B

Moses

'If your Presence does not go with us, do not send us up from here. How will anyone know that you are pleased with me and with your people unless you go with us? What else will distinguish me and your people from all the other people on the face of the earth?'

I once pinned a paper geranium to Margaret Thatcher's overcoat. It was 'Geranium Day', a fundraising initiative of the Royal National Institute of the Blind, and I was the lucky youngster who got to affix the flower to the most photographed lapel in the nation. What I remember most clearly, though, is the elderly blind woman who had the privilege of holding the collecting box. As Mrs Thatcher put her coins in the slot, Winnie took her to task, chastising her for going to bed too late and not looking after herself properly. I was gobsmacked that someone would speak to a real live prime minister in that way.

Without wishing to liken Baroness Thatcher to the Almighty, I remember being similarly gobsmacked the first time I read this prayer of Moses. How did he have the nerve to challenge God so openly? How did he dare question Almighty God's plans and try to set conditions for him in that way? Yet Moses' prayer was nothing short of destiny-shaping for Israel. Had he not prayed it so boldly, who knows what their future might have been, travelling into an unknown land and setting up a whole new society without their God in their midst.

Sometimes our prayers need to be uncomfortably bold and confrontational. We can take reassurance from the fact that Moses wasn't smitten for his audacity: in fact, God seems to have welcomed his impassioned intervention. Ultimately, God is looking for partners in the work of his kingdom. He is looking for people who care enough to get frustrated when things don't seem to be going in the right direction. He is seeking out moved and motivated people like Moses, who will wrestle with him for the good of those to whom they are called.

....

What do you get most uptight about? What stirs you up? Have you ever taken God to task over it? If not, why not give it a go? He is big enough to handle it.

                                                                                    LYNDALL B

Hannah

In bitterness of soul Hannah wept much and prayed to the Lord.

My family heritage is Italian and, although we have only ever lived in the UK, I did spend many a childhood holiday in that beautiful country. I loved almost everything about it—the food and the beaches and the weather—but one thing used to disturb me greatly and that was the loudness. I would listen to a veritable tirade of conversation, all delivered at high volume with considerable aggression, and would retreat hastily into the background for fear of imminent explosion— only to be told by my Italian-speaking mother that the speakers were merely discussing the weather. It seemed that no topic of conversation could be tackled without passion turned up to the max.

In our Western church culture, prayer seems to have been turned down to acceptable levels of politeness. It is often organised into tidy phrases and delivered in subdued tones, so Hannah is something of a refreshing change. For her, prayer was anything but polite. She was utterly desperate and so was her prayer. In fact, so 'inappropriate' was her demeanour, that day in the temple, that Eli the high priest nearly threw her out altogether.

Prayer devoid of emotion is prayer without life. Raw and untidy though our emotions may be at times, they are part of our God-inspired design and they are a crucial part of our prayers. Not only is God the provider who wants to meet our needs; he is also the lover who longs to connect with us in our deepest thoughts and feelings.

As you embark on prayer today, why not choose to express to God a Hannah prayer—not just a recital of your needs but also a passionate, untidy outburst of your deepest longings, for yourself, for your family and for your community.

....

If you were only allowed one prayer to pray, what would that prayer be? Let the answer come not from your mind but from your heart.

LYNDALL B

Nicodemus

[Nicodemus] came to Jesus at night and said, 'Rabbi, we know you are a teacher who has come from God. For no one could perform the miraculous signs you are doing if God were not with him.'

Have you ever wanted to derail a church meeting? Perhaps it was a Bible study and you wanted to ask a really tricky, controversial question; or perhaps it was a sermon and you wanted to disagree violently with the preacher; or perhaps—horror of horrors—it was a prayer meeting and you wanted to stand up, throw your Bible on the floor and shout at the top of your voice, 'What if God doesn't answer prayer?' If you have ever wanted to do that, then you are a hero in the order of Nicodemus.

Calling disciples had been a pretty simple business for Jesus so far. The fishermen had more or less dropped their nets on the spot and followed him. The crowds were even beginning to flock to him. Nicodemus was a different matter. He wasn't going to be an easy win. He needed answers before he would commit himself to this new rabbi on the block.

What was Jesus' response? Was it to tell him to stop thinking and start believing? Was it to chastise him for needing to know the things of God? No, it was simply to receive him, questions and all. Jesus wasn't too afraid or too offended to have the conversation; in fact, again, he seemed to positively welcome it.

Whether you are the kind of person who only ever questions matters of faith in your darkest hour or whether your mind seems to be a perpetually seething mass of doubts, know today that God loves and values thinkers. He made the mind and he made the universe that poses us so many insoluble conundrums, and he is thrilled when we let the one grapple with the other.

The only proviso he makes is that we let him into the conversation.

....

Is there a question you are too afraid to ask God?

LYNDALL B

Paul

I keep asking that the God of our Lord Jesus Christ, the glorious Father, may give you the Spirit of wisdom and revelation, so that you may know him better.

I never knew you could be passionate about welding. I was studying technical translation at university and our course leaders decided it would be a good idea to provide us with a basic induction to all things engineering, so we headed down to the local further education college to visit the welding department. As I am blind, they didn't consider it a good idea to let me have a go myself, but by the end of the session I was quite infected by the joys of fusing metals, such was the passion and eloquence of the man who was teaching us.

If you want to learn something, don't just read a book about it; find an expert to teach you. When we know about a subject, we can be informative about it, but when we understand something inside out, we pass it on with real conviction and love.

Paul was a pioneer in his field. He didn't have the benefit of centuries of Christian tradition behind him. All he had was a rather dramatic encounter with Jesus and the dawning realisation that this ordinary-looking Galilean had just turned the tide of history. He travelled the region, teaching this very new good news, but he can only have been half a step ahead himself. The truths he was teaching were ones that he himself had only just absorbed.

It is as though Paul's prayer life reflects this immediacy. When he turns to prayer for the churches he has planted, there is a longing beneath the surface of his words—an urgency that these new believers should grasp the wonder and the joy of what he himself has discovered in Jesus.

When we allow the things God is teaching us to flow out into our prayers for others, our intercession takes on new life and passion.

....

Which truth about Jesus has struck you most profoundly recently? As you pray for people today, pray that they will discover this truth for themselves.

LYNDALL B

73

Joshua

Then the Lord said to Joshua, 'See, I have delivered Jericho into your hands, along with its king and its fighting men.'

Let's be honest: we've all done it, haven't we? We've read through a set of simple-looking instructions to build something, failed to follow them to the letter and ended up with an object that doesn't look anything like how it was meant to look. If you want to achieve a certain result, you need to follow the maker's instructions faithfully and accurately.

Joshua's prayer time on the plain outside Jericho is my idea of a dream come true. Before him stood the most impenetrable city in Canaan and he needed a plan for conquering it. Then the 'commander of the army of the Lord' arrived and delivered him a set of instructions that were so clear, they would put the paperwork for a flatpack wardrobe to shame. All he had to do was follow them to the letter and the city would fall effortlessly into his hands.

If only it were that simple for us! If only we could present the Lord with our day's dilemmas and download the answers from him in words of two syllables or less. Before you begin to feel inadequate for not sharing Joshua's experience, though, let me remind you of his history. Joshua had been Moses' assistant and there could have been few greater mentors than Moses. Yet we read in Exodus 33:11 that, having spoken with God, Moses would leave the tent of meeting but Joshua would stay. By the time he arrived at Jericho's plain, Joshua had spent hours and hours, day after day, in the presence of God.

Listening to God isn't a complicated business, but we do need to get to know his voice. When Joshua got his Jericho instructions, the encounter was full of awe and reverence, but at heart it was an encounter with a friend he knew well. Answers in life come from intimacy with our Maker.

....

Gracious and compassionate God, as I lay before you the struggles and unanswered questions in my life, I rest for a moment in your presence. Though I long to know the answers to my questions, my greater longing is to know you and to recognise your voice. Amen

LYNDALL B

Elisha

**And Elisha prayed, 'O Lord, open his eyes so that he may see.'
Then the Lord opened the servant's eyes, and he looked and saw
the hills full of horses and chariots of fire all around Elisha.**

The story is told of a man who visited a building site where three
stonemasons were hard at work, each carving a block of stone. He
asked each of them the same question: 'What are you doing?'

The first replied, 'I am carving this stone.' The second replied, 'I
am building a wall.' The third replied, 'I am building a cathedral.'

Some people are inspiring to be with, because they can look
beyond the discouragement and drudgery of their circumstances and
catch a glimpse of the bigger picture of which they're a part. Elisha's
servant needed that kind of sight. All he could see were the physical things—the army surrounding the city. He needed to see beyond
the visible into the invisible. Elisha's ministry was marked by authority. The Bible tells of many occasions when people's circumstances
turned around completely as a result of Elisha's prayers. Pools of
water appeared in the desert; dead people came to life. Elisha's prayer
life literally brought the impossible into the realm of the possible.

I used to wonder if I would grow out of my youthful fervour for
intercessory prayer—those heady days when I believed everything
was possible if we just asked God for it. Many years and hundreds of
unanswered prayers later, I sincerely hope I never do. Elisha's servant
needed to know that the story was not as bleak as it seemed, and our
world still needs to know that there is a God who can undo the most
terrible evil and make life and hope out of absolutely nothing.

Elisha made it all look rather easy. In my experience, break-
throughs come packaged in much unanswered prayer, but come they
do; and, when we press in to God in faith, we find that the impossible really is possible.

....

*Father God, I give you my flagging faith and trailing disappointments.
You haven't always done things the way I would have liked and I
haven't always believed in your goodness. Today, enlarge my vision to
see your reality and believe for the impossible; fire up my faith again!*

LYNDALL B

Ali Herbert writes:

When you think about the word 'worship', what does it mean to you? Does it mean a young man at the front strumming a guitar or an organ pumping out a much-loved recital? Does it mean sitting staring into a candle flame, catching a moment of peace and solitude? In its fullest form, worship is what we are called to do with our entire lives; it is our response to God—with our relationships, our time, our money, our attitudes and so on. The Westminster Shorter Catechism begins with this: 'Man's [or Woman's] chief end is to glorify God and enjoy him for ever.' While that statement doesn't use the exact word 'worship', it is a great definition of what worship is—a true response to God's power, majesty and great love and mercy towards us.

If you're feeling a bit short-changed by the fact that sometimes we collapse this huge idea into a 20-minute slot of singing, remember that the wonderful experience of music and voice is God-given and has certainly been used throughout history to give glory back to God. Singing and praying together as a church and family is a wonderful way to focus on God and his character. It's a great way to learn words of scripture, to define our theology and to do something truly communal. Music has a beautiful power to draw us in and soften us and we should certainly continue to explore different varieties of the 'art of noise' as we worship God. But remember, too, that this is only one part of our lifelong call to worship a mighty God.

Over the next couple of weeks, we'll be looking at some examples of worship and song in the Bible, some old hymns, some new lyrics, how and why we worship, who we worship and some inspiring women worshippers. It is all about a response to a mighty God who is interested in you!

Who is a worshipper?

For by [Christ] all things were created: things in heaven and on earth, visible and invisible, whether thrones or powers or rulers or authorities; all things were created by him and for him.

You are a worshipper. We are all worshippers: it's what we were made to do. Even people who wouldn't call themselves Christians are worshippers: everybody worships something or someone. Whatever it is that we value most—ourselves, a relationship, a career, a football team, an object—that is what we worship. If we choose not to worship God, we'll simply worship something else instead.

Michael Jackson was an extraordinary entertainer but he was not a god. However, if you ever watch any footage of one of his concerts, you will see an image of misplaced 'worship': people have their eyes closed or they gaze adoringly upwards, arms raised, swaying, giving glory to someone who was a fragile human like the rest of us. This is some kind of worship, although, sadly, aimed at someone who would never have been able to bring the redemption we all need.

In huge contrast, we know the Lord, Jesus Christ, who offers to come and live in our hearts and bring us freedom from all that would seek to damage or oppress us in this world—including death. That is good news! We were made by him and for him, to enjoy him and worship him and live for him. Today's reading gives us a good idea of why we are worshipping God—who he is and what he's done. There's a reason why we are to put God above everything else. Graham Kendrick's song 'The Servant King' sums it up so well. The all-powerful Creator of the universe surrendered himself to death on the cross. Today, let's give God his worth.

....

Take a moment to praise the God who made everything in the world around us—from atoms to stars.

                                                                ALI H

Hallelujah!

Praise God in his sanctuary; praise him in his mighty heavens.
Praise him for his acts of power; praise him for his surpassing
greatness... Let everything that has breath praise the Lord. Praise
the Lord.

Well, that's clear, then! A set of notes on worship would be sadly
incomplete without at least one psalm. I've read that Billy Graham
would read five psalms each day to get through the book every
month, and it seems to have worked well for him! These 150 songs
are literally at the centre of the Bible and they praise God and cry out
to God in many different situations and for many reasons, but number 150 is the final psalm and the one that focuses entirely on God's
greatness and nothing else. You can hear joy and delight in every sen-
tence. Whichever way you worship God—with tambourines, strings,
cymbals, dancing, speaking, singing or silence—it doesn't matter. Just
do it!

In the Hebrew Bible, the word translated here as 'Praise the Lord'
is actually the word 'Hallelujah': 'Halel' means to tell someone they
are great, 'u' means all of you and 'jah' means the Lord. So the word
is literally saying: tell God he's the best! The psalm also mentions the
sanctuary, the place where we gather with other believers to meet
with God; and praising and worshipping God is our reason for gathering together. It's the reason you are reading these notes, the reason
we go to church and the real reason we exist. It doesn't matter what
instruments we choose to use to praise God, or how we like to sing,
speak, be silent, dance or move, it just matters that we do it, that we
praise God for who he is, for what he has done for us and for the
promises he has given us. By the way, singing in church is not for the
singers; singing in church is for the believers. Praise the Lord, praise
the Lord, praise the Lord!

....

*'Through Jesus, therefore, let us continually offer to God a sacrifice
of praise—the fruit of lips that confess his name' (Hebrews 13:15).*

ALI H

An unlikely candidate

'Yet a time is coming and has now come when the true worshippers will worship the Father in spirit and truth, for they are the kind of worshippers the Father seeks. God is spirit, and his worshippers must worship in spirit and in truth.'

My grandmother told me a story. A little boy was sitting in an old church, surrounded by well-dressed people. The organ started playing and the people stood and sang loudly and briskly. It made a glorious sound. Suddenly an angel whisked the little boy up into heaven, where he could look down on the assembled congregation. To his surprise, while he could see the people's mouths opening and closing, he could hear no sound coming out, apart from the rather croaky and out-of-tune voice of a little old lady in the pew furthest from the front. The boy thought this odd and turned to the angel with a questioning look. The angel smiled at him and said, 'Ah, up here we can only hear the ones who actually mean what they say.' Now I don't know if that's how it is to God, but in our verses today Jesus teaches that meaningful worship must be authentic and inspired by the Spirit. God is looking at the heart of each person, not the outward show of skill, confidence or talent.

The woman at the well in today's reading is a great example of this. She was an outcast from her community—which is why she was fetching water alone, at the hottest part of the day—and, according to the laws of the day, Jesus shouldn't even have spoken with her. He saw her life in all its brokenness and her open heart, however, and she responded to him by believing immediately and calling her whole village to meet him. God uses unlikely people who know that they need to rely on him and know just how much he has given them. Those people will worship him wholeheartedly, in the Spirit and for real.

....

Spend a little time before God, being honest with him.

ALI H

What God has done for us

All this is for your benefit, so that the grace that is reaching more and more people may cause thanksgiving to overflow to the glory of God.

One of the most famous hymns in English—and the one most beloved of wedding parties—is 'Amazing Grace', written over 230 years ago by John Newton, an ex-slave trader. It reminds us again and again of the grace that Paul speaks about in our verses today, through which God, in Jesus, has reached down to us in our brokenness and lifted us up into healing and life in all its fullness. Spend a few moments bringing these famous words about grace alive again for yourself:

Amazing Grace, how sweet the sound
That saved a wretch like me.
I once was lost but now am found,
Was blind but now I see.

'Twas Grace that taught my heart to fear,
And Grace my fears relieved.
How precious did that Grace appear,
The hour I first believed.

Through many dangers, toils and snares
We have already come.
'Twas Grace that brought us safe thus far,
And Grace will lead us home.

When we've been there ten thousand years,
Bright shining as the sun,
We've no less days to sing God's praise
Than when we've first begun.

....

Father, thank you for saving me from the consequences of my sin.
Thank you for working in me, by your Holy Spirit, to transform so
that I can be more like Jesus.

ALI H

Women of worship: Miriam

Miriam sang to them: 'Sing to the Lord, for he is highly exalted. The horse and its rider he has hurled into the sea.'

We are so used to the idea that communal worship in the Bible is led by men (the priests), we forget that there are some magnificent women who step forward with a song to the Lord. Over the next few days we will look at some of them.

Miriam is the first female worship leader we meet in the Bible and her song is an immediate reaction to the miracle of the parting of the Red Sea. You can read the full story in Exodus 3—14. Miriam had a difficult life: she was born into slavery in Egypt, witnessing the harsh realities of life as an immigrant under an unsympathetic Pharaoh, watching her people suffering and dying, then experiencing the wild hope and fear of their escape towards the promised land. As she and her people stand by the swirling waters of the Red Sea, though, she doesn't look back in bitterness. Instead she steps forward with what she has—her voice and a tambourine—to give the glory to God. She doesn't look for recompense or even an understanding of what she has been through but simply chooses to praise the one who has saved her.

This is quite a challenge to us as we go through both good and bad times. Will we choose to keep praising God or blame him for our circumstances? Will we choose to hold on to the hurt or let it go in his presence? To worship is definitely a choice. Whatever circumstances you are facing, ask God to help you praise him, letting go of hurts and disappointments, receiving healing and fresh hope from our loving God. He is able to work in even the bleakest situation for your good.

....

Lord, I choose to turn to you, to worship you. You never leave me. Your love amazes me. Thank you for giving me hope and promising me a future.

ALI H

Women of worship: Hannah

There is no one holy like the Lord; there is no one besides you; there is no Rock like our God.

Hannah was another woman who knew about suffering and disappointment: in 1:15 she describes herself as 'deeply troubled'. In 1 Samuel 1, we read that, although she had a kind and loving husband, she was unable to conceive, leading to a sadness that was exacerbated by the taunting of her husband's second wife. In those times, children gave a woman her worth. Fortunately, in our culture, this is no longer the case; however, even now, the experience of miscarriage, infertility or the lack of a suitable partner can strike deep into our hearts, even to the core of our identity.

I have two young children but I have experienced two miscarriages: they were not physically painful but were difficult emotionally. I have friends who are coming to terms with the likelihood of never having children and some who have lost babies in late pregnancy or after the birth. These are traumatic situations, often made worse by a sense of guilt and shame. Hannah's response was to take her bitterness to the Lord, not covering up her feelings but openly expressing her distress (1:11–15). She models for us a way to be totally real in the presence of God, a God who promises us healing and restoration and will stand with us and for us, whatever our circumstances.

God mercifully gave Hannah the son she so longed for; in return, her worship was to give this precious son back to God—a wonderful act of sacrificial thanksgiving. This was Hannah's journey from distress to rejoicing: she had a broken heart; she turned, in her hurt, towards God; he offered his grace and mercy and she answered with sacrifice and praise.

Hannah's broken heart is healed and the first words of her next song of worship are 'My heart rejoices in the Lord' (2:1).

....

Pray for someone who is struggling with issues of childlessness today—or for someone in the middle of parenting young children.

ALI H

Women of worship: Deborah

On that day Deborah and Barak son of Abinoam sang this song:
'When the princes in Israel take the lead, when the people willingly
offer themselves—praise the Lord! Hear this, you kings! Listen,
you rulers! I will sing to the Lord, I will sing; I will make music to
the Lord, the God of Israel.'

There are some wonderful women in the Bible, but none is quite
as feisty as Deborah! Her story is told in Judges 4 and 5, when she
is shown as the leader of Israel. Her people, as so often, are under
threat from the Canaanites and, in particular, from Sisera, the feared
commander of the Canaanite army. Deborah, who is described as a
'prophetess' as well as a 'wife' (4:4), discerns God's will that Barak,
her army commander, should defeat this enemy. Unfortunately, Barak
decides he needs some hand-holding from Deborah and refuses to
go on his own. He therefore misses out on the full blessing and the
victory is given to Deborah and another woman called Jael, who
eventually kills Sisera in his sleep with a tent-peg and hammer. You
wouldn't want to get on the wrong side of these women!

Deborah is an encouragement to us as we juggle the different
aspects of our lives. She is definitely feminine and calls herself the
'mother of Israel' (v. 7) as well as being a wife. However, she is not
afraid to take on the traditional male role of leading an army and a
country, and is entirely dependent on hearing God's voice for her
wisdom, action and decisions. The whole of Judges 5 is an outpouring of praise to God entitled 'The song of Deborah'. She knows that
if she wants to continue to be in the centre of God's will, she needs
to be leaning on him, worshipping him, giving all the honour back to
him and listening to him. What a great role model she is for us and
what an encouragement as we step out into today and all that it holds
in store. Avoid Jael's tent-pegs though!

....

*Lord, I often have to fulfil so many different roles. Give me the grace
and mercy and energy I need, and the wisdom to stop and listen to
your voice.*

ALI H

Women of worship: Mary

'My soul glorifies the Lord and my spirit rejoices in God my Saviour, for he has been mindful of the humble state of his servant. From now on all generations will call me blessed, for the Mighty One has done great things for me—holy is his name.'

A pregnant, unmarried, teenage, poor Middle Eastern girl called Mary goes to visit her cousin Elizabeth, who is also pregnant, and something extraordinary happens. Elizabeth's baby leaps in her womb and both women are overwhelmed with delight, crying out prophetically. Mary's response is to sing this fantastic song that we know as the Magnificat, an outpouring of gratitude to the Lord who, she says, 'has done great things for me'.

Now let's just pause and rewind. Remember the circumstance Mary has found herself in? Yet she sings from her heart and soul about mercy and blessing and help. She remembers the things God has done for her people and the promises he has made and can't stop herself from singing out loud, joyously and extravagantly. Her life may be precarious, with little in the way of comforts and luxuries, but her worship is unstoppable. Can we be too comfortable sometimes? Can we rely on our own money and wisdom and become too self-reliant? Do we find it difficult to sing along with Mary, who is aware of her frailty? Perhaps it's good to remember that, throughout the Bible, it is the humble who are lifted up, those who know they truly rely on the Lord. Of course, being wealthy or comfortable doesn't mean that God rejects us, but it does mean we need to continue to humble ourselves before the 'Mighty One', to remember where the glory belongs and be thankful for the abundance we have.

....

Speak or sing out loud a list of the many things in your life that you are thankful to God for—from family to food to hot showers and warm duvets.

ALI H

Because you're worth it

Then Mary took about a pint of pure nard, an expensive perfume; she poured it on Jesus' feet and wiped his feet with her hair. And the house was filled with the fragrance of the perfume.

Do you ever play that game where you decide who your perfect dinner party guests would be? Apparently Stephen Fry is top of the list in most surveys taken. The party we read about here, though, must have topped them all for an unusual mix of guests. First of all, we have Jesus the wandering miracle-maker who claims to be the Son of God, we have Lazarus, recently raised from the dead (quite a talking point, you would think), we have Mary and we also have Judas Iscariot, who is about to betray Jesus. This party must have been simmering with anticipation, wonder, emotion and tension, and it becomes the trigger point that ultimately leads to Jesus' death.

Mary's act of true and extravagant worship is too much for Judas. He is offended by the pointlessness (as he sees it) of her act (v. 5). This is where the countdown begins, but Mary knows none of this as she enters the room, about to risk possible rejection and certainly risking looking crazy. Her perfume is worth a year's wages—perhaps £20,000 in today's money—but she knows that it is a fraction of what Jesus is worth, a fraction of what he has given to her. Jesus loves what Mary does for him. He accepts the tears and perfume graciously and wholeheartedly.

This is such a beautiful picture of God receiving our worship—not just our songs but also our words, our decisions, our private lives. Nothing we do will go unnoticed by God, and he is touched and blessed and moved by our worship. It blesses him—and your life is worth so much more to him than that bottle of perfume.

....

'But thanks be to God, who always leads us in triumphal procession in Christ and through us spreads everywhere the fragrance of the knowledge of him' (2 Corinthians 2:14).

ALI H

A participation sport?

David, wearing a linen ephod, danced before the Lord with all his might, while he and the entire house of Israel brought up the ark of the Lord with shouts and the sound of trumpets.

So what makes a good worshipper? King David was described as a man after God's own heart (1 Samuel 13:14) and he was notorious for dancing publicly in his underwear. How would you feel about somebody doing that in your own church setting? Later, the priests and people in the temple fell down to the ground because the glory of the Lord was so heavy in there (2 Chronicles 7:2–3).

Now I'm not saying that we should all go to church, dance wildly, hold our arms in the air or fall prostrate on the ground—although many do express their worship in those ways. But I do believe that, first, we should be seeking the passion that David had and, second, we should be very careful about judging how others choose to worship God.

Michal, David's wife, despised her husband and made the mistake of believing that David's dignity and status were of more importance than his heart for God. Do we make that mistake, too? For the sake of our 'dignity', do we mute our worship and hide our heart for God? Perhaps you long to be freer in your worship but find it too hard in front of others at church. Could you be freer at home before an audience of one, the Lord? He delights in every expression of worship when it is honest and led by the Spirit. Can we also make a decision not to judge how other people worship, whether freely or formally? We don't know what is in their hearts, just as they don't know what is in ours. Church should be a place where we can be vulnerable and feel safe, and an attitude that refuses to judge others can at least begin with us. Perhaps it's good for all of us to try forms of worship that are outside our comfort zone.

....

Would I feel free to dance or move to music alone in my own room as an act of worship? Dare I try an extended period of silence, listening to the Lord?

ALI H

Fighting back

Again, the devil took him to a very high mountain... 'All this I will give you,' he said, 'if you will bow down and worship me.' Jesus said to him, 'Away from me, Satan! For it is written: "Worship the Lord your God, and serve him only."'

Every day there is a battle for your worship. While we don't want to obsess about spiritual warfare rather than focusing on Jesus, we need to remember that temptation is not just about a nice cream cake but, rather, a serious spiritual reality. We are constantly tempted to spend our time, money and desire on things and people that will not fulfil us, to the detriment of storing up 'treasure in heaven' (Matthew 6:20).

Even the biggest celebrities could tell us that these false treasures won't satisfy. I think it was Robbie Williams who said, 'I got to the top, but when I got to the top, there was nothing there...' The philosopher Pascal called it the 'God-shaped vacuum' in us, which nothing but God can fill.

The temptation to worship outside God's boundaries is strong and this war has been raging since before time. The story of Satan is one of twisted worship, of a being that decided that worship belonged to itself and not to God. In our verses today we see a continuation of that story—Satan wanting Jesus to worship him. What a victory that would have been for him and what a disaster for us! Satan shows Jesus all the world can offer: Jesus knows without a doubt that not only will it not fulfil him, but there is something far bigger at stake. Jesus answers Satan brilliantly, using Bible verses to combat that persuasive whisper. He tells Satan in no uncertain words that worship belongs to the Lord God. When material temptations or negative desires come knocking at our doors (and they will), let's follow Jesus' example of deflecting them with truth from the Bible and making a decision to worship God instead. Worship is the best weapon we have!

....

Tell God the temptations you struggle with and then spend some time worshipping him. Perhaps read a psalm or two out loud as a reminder of whom we worship.

ALI H

Keeping your word

O Lord, you are my God; I will exalt you and praise your name, for in perfect faithfulness you have done marvellous things, things planned long ago.

A few years ago, I was standing and worshipping in our church and I was pregnant. My husband and I hadn't told anyone about the pregnancy at this point, but a friend of mine leaned over during the singing and asked if I was. I was taken aback, but she said that God had given her a vivid dream of me holding a baby. I felt reassured and pleased at God's word. A couple of weeks later I had a miscarriage.

In the middle of my disappointment was a question: 'Why did God seem to promise me this child?' However, as I trusted the wisdom of the friend who had spoken to me, I held on to her words. A couple of months later I became pregnant again and had a somewhat rollercoaster pregnancy, culminating in my son's birth, six weeks early—but everything was fine and my son quickly thrived. I now see my friend's word as a promise from God that he fulfilled in a wonderful way, even though not necessarily in the way I had expected.

Our verses today speak about a God who keeps his word. They speak about a God who has good plans for us, who is a refuge when we need him and a powerful advocate. They also speak of a God who wants to celebrate with us, who will destroy our sufferings and hurt, who will entirely wipe out death. At the end of verse 8 are the words, 'The Lord has spoken.' I love the certainty in that! God promises many good things to us, and when we see those promises fulfilled we will be able to say with our own certainty, 'This is the Lord, we trusted in him; let us rejoice and be glad in his salvation' (v. 9).

....

Are there things in your life that you need to trust God with, or fulfilled promises you want to celebrate?

ALI H

Seen through a child's eyes

And [Jesus] said: 'I tell you the truth, unless you change and become like little children, you will never enter the kingdom of heaven. Therefore those who humble themselves like this child are the greatest in the kingdom of heaven.'

Isn't it interesting that some of the most powerful, memorable and theologically sound songs we sing in church are the children's songs? Do you remember the song 'Jesus loves the little children' or 'Jesus' love is very wonderful' or perhaps 'Wide, wide as the ocean, high as the heavens above'? It's amazing how these songs remain clear in our minds even after many years.

I suppose it's not surprising that these songs are profound, though, as Jesus told us quite clearly that we need to be like little children to enter the kingdom of heaven. The problem is, we complicate things so much as we get older. We debate questions that can't be answered this side of heaven; we question our hearts; we get distracted by the foibles of others around us. We get caught up in the hows and whys and wherefores. Of course I believe that God has given us our minds to use and I also believe that we should continue to challenge our preconceptions and explore as much of God and his kingdom as we can, but the central message of the gospel is so simple that a child can understand it—and sing about it.

Dr Karl Barth was one of the 20th century's most well-known and distinguished intellectuals. He wrote many volumes on the meaning of life and faith. Asked once if he could sum up his life's work, he thought for a moment and said, 'Jesus loves me; this I know, for the Bible tells me so.' Enough said.

....

Jesus loves me; this I know, for the Bible tells me so. Little ones to him belong; they are weak, but he is strong.

ANNA BARTLETT WARNER/WILLIAM BRADBURY, *THE EVANGELICAL CHURCH SCHOOL HYMNAL*, 1931

ALI H

Heavenly worship

Then I looked and heard the voice of many angels, numbering thousands upon thousands, and ten thousand times ten thousand. They encircled the throne and the living creatures and the elders.

To finish this series of notes exploring worship, there really is no alternative but to look at the book of Revelation. The book was written by John in his elder years and describes a vision he had on the Island of Patmos. It is a fascinating, bewildering, vivid and wild glimpse of heaven. It's often a book that frightens people who take it literally, but when we see it as an image, a poem or a description (as near as words can take us) of the indescribable, then it becomes more accessible.

In chapter 4, John describes the throne of heaven and the incredible colours and lights and noises he experiences. As we move into chapter 5, we see the centrepiece of all this drama and spectacle… and it is a vulnerable lamb—Jesus in his rightful place. Around the lamb are countless angels singing 'a new song' on a breathtaking scale. 'Worthy,' they sing, 'honour', 'glory', 'praise' and 'power', and together with the elders they fall down and worship with their bodies, too. Wow!

This passage serves to remind us that our worship is part of something far more spectacular and universal than we can possibly imagine. Our living worship should reflect it as best we can—the splendour of Jesus, the majesty, the intimacy, the sacrifice. One day we will see and understand worship totally and be able to worship him perfectly, but for now we have this striking and mindblowing glimpse of what will be. The best is yet to come!

....

Worship the Lord with all your heart, all your mind and all your strength, and worship him in spirit and in truth.

ALI H

Jean Watson writes:

Who do you think you are? How well do you know yourself? Does self-knowledge matter? Because I think it does, I want to have a look at some people in the Bible and the impact of their characters within God's plans.

There's a very old verse that goes like this:

Sow a thought and you reap an act,
Sow an act and you reap a habit,
Sow a habit and you reap a character,
Sow a character and you reap a destiny.
CHARLES READE (1814–84)

That's putting it a bit simplistically and starkly, maybe, but there is here, I think, a general truth about actions and consequences and about who we are as individuals, affecting the course of our own and other people's lives.

Back to our question: does self-knowledge matter? Yes, because knowing ourselves means we can be more consistent and thoughtful in our choices and actions, as well as more understanding of others. These benefits cannot fail to have positive consequences and, within God's plans, can alter the course of our own and other people's lives and futures for good—and for eternity.

So let's have a look at some biblical people and think about our own characters and characteristics and their potential impact.

Lovingly loyal Ruth

Ruth replied, '… Where you go I will go, and where you stay I will stay. Your people will be my people and your God my God. Where you die I will die, and there I will be buried.'

Three widows—Naomi and her two Moabite daughters-in-law, Orpah and Ruth—set out from Moab to Bethlehem. Naomi urges her loyal companions to return to Moab in the hope of remarriage. Orpah, weeping and reluctantly, bids the other two goodbye and leaves, but Ruth refuses to leave Naomi, who has lost not only her husband but both her sons as well.

What stands out for me in the character of Ruth is her committed loyalty: unusually, perhaps, towards her mother-in-law! The words she uses have become famous throughout the world as a very beautiful and complete expression of loving loyalty. The word 'loving' here is important because loyalty can spring from a sense of duty and be offered in a cold or grudging spirit. When that happens, it blesses neither the recipient nor the giver.

Ruth's loyalty sprang from her loving heart and showed itself in all that she said and did subsequently, which we will be looking at in more detail tomorrow. For today, think about how far out of her comfort zone she was prepared to go—to a strange land, among a strange people with a strange culture.

I can think of some examples in my life when my loving loyalty has taken me out of my comfort zone. I have found it hard at the time, but later, in reflecting on such times, I have been pleased about what I have managed do, with help, and about what I have learnt.

When has your loving loyalty taken you out of your comfort zone and what was the outcome for you and for others? Perhaps you are facing a Ruth-type situation now. Take it, along with your feelings about it, to God in prayer.

JEAN W

Sow a character, reap a destiny: Ruth

So Boaz took Ruth and she became his wife. When he made love to her, the Lord enabled her to conceive, and she gave birth to a son.

If you can read or scan the chapters between yesterday's and today's readings, you will see how the story develops.

Ruth gleans in the fields and makes a favourable impression on everyone, including Boaz, a relative of Naomi's late husband Elimelek. Naomi tells Ruth to 'ask' indirectly for Boaz in marriage, in keeping with a law that allowed a husband's relative to marry and give an heir to a childless woman. Quietly and without drawing unnecessary attention to herself or making things awkward for Boaz, Ruth does as she is asked. Boaz willingly takes on his responsibilities, sorts out the proper way of doing things with another relative and marries Ruth, bringing an end to Ruth's childlessness. Naomi is grandchildless no longer!

From every chapter Ruth's character shines out—her love for and risk-taking obedience to Naomi; her willingness to work hard and fit in; her tact, courtesy and humility.

What resulted from Ruth's character and actions within God's plans? A change of destiny for herself and her mother-in-law, which was to have cosmic consequences. She and Boaz had a son and from his line came King David. Glance through the genealogy in Matthew 1 and you will see that from David's line came great David's greater son, Jesus; and the cosmic consequences of his life, death and resurrection have filtered down to me, writing these notes, and to you, reading them.

···

Can you identify some of your characteristics and the effects they have had or are having on your and other people's lives, for better or worse?

JEAN W

A volatile temperament: Elijah

'Let it be known today that you are God in Israel and that I am your servant… Take my life; I am no better than my ancestors.'

Try to read or at least scan both these passages to pick out aspects of Elijah's personality. I think you'll agree that here we see a very human prophet—on a high one moment and suicidally low the next. First he stages an impressive contest between God and his prophet (singular) and Baal and his prophets (plural). Elijah must have had enormous confidence in God to mastermind such a public event—one in which he would have looked a complete idiot if things had gone wrong. But the fire of the Lord fell and the people were awestruck and cried out, 'The Lord—he is God!' (18:39). Elijah must have been on cloud nine.

Then he learns of Jezebel's plans to kill him and his mood plummets. He runs away into the desert, hides under a bush and wishes to die. God meets him where he is—worn out, hungry and frightened—and provides food, rest and work to do, along with the assurance that he is not alone as a prophet of the true God.

Was Elijah bipolar? We don't know, but he certainly had his ups and downs. Our moods may or may not be as extreme as his were, but we all have them, surely.

I find it reassuring that God accepts and uses Elijah just as he is. He honours his faith in the 'up' moments and draws alongside him in the 'down' ones. Perhaps you can identify with me when I say that I do not have visible, tangible, audible evidences of God's presence and activity in the way that Elijah did. So I have to keep trying to walk by faith rather than sight and to experience God in new and different ways—or not at all—in such times.

....

Reflect on your ups and downs and how you have experienced God in them.

JEAN W

Unlucky in love: Leah

When the Lord saw that Leah was not loved, he enabled her to conceive.

I wanted to include Leah in these notes because I know people who feel very much as Leah might well have felt—passed over; in the shadow of someone else; always last to be picked for a team.

Whatever 'weak eyes' meant (v. 17), they weren't attractive. It must have been very hard for Leah to have a beautiful younger sister. It strikes me that she could well have had low self-worth. Otherwise, why would she have agreed to her father's humiliating plan to trick Jacob into marrying her? She probably felt, as Laban evidently did, that this would be her best chance of getting married—which was vitally important for a woman in those days. How she must have dreaded the morning after the wedding night, when all would be revealed and Jacob would be furious!

Afterwards, did she meekly accept her position as the unloved wife or burn with jealousy or nurse deep hurt? We don't know. Our reading today tells us that Leah was not loved. She was not loved by Jacob, but she certainly was by God and, we hope, by the many children he blessed her with. The presence and love of her many children perhaps brought her the fulfilment and satisfaction that she didn't find elsewhere.

It is great to know that God loves us. God's love reached Leah through his gift of children to her, but God's love can reach us in all sorts of other ways, too. It can reach us through human love and friendship, so that we feel valued and have a sense of belonging. It can also reach us through work, creativity, medicine and all the other fruits of human skill and knowledge that affect our physical, psychological and spiritual well-being.

....

How is God's love being made flesh in your life? How are you making God's love flesh in other people's lives?

JEAN W

Sceptical but not cynical: Thomas

'Unless I see the nail marks in his hands and put my finger where
the nails were, and put my hand into his side, I will not believe...
My Lord and my God!'

Can you identify with Thomas in this story? The disciples tell him
they have seen Jesus. He replies that unless he too can see and touch
Jesus, he won't believe. Wouldn't we have felt and spoken as he
did? After all, resurrection from the dead must have seemed highly
unlikely, if not impossible, to him.

Anyway, Jesus comes and invites Thomas to see his scarred hands
and put his hand into his wounded side. Thomas responds in awed
faith and worship: 'My Lord and my God!'

I think that Thomas was sceptical rather than cynical. According
to one dictionary the former means 'inclined towards incredulity',
whereas the latter means 'disinclined to believe in goodness or self-
lessness'. In this flawed world and life, I think we need sometimes to
be sceptical but not cynical. It's not wrong to want evidence before
believing something way beyond our experience and hence incredible to us; we are told by Jesus to be 'as shrewd as snakes and as
innocent as doves' (Matthew 10:16).

In this story, Jesus gives Thomas the proof he asks for and Thomas'
scepticism willingly melts before his experience in the actual presence of Jesus. Jesus adds, though, that those who have not seen him
as Thomas has seen him, and yet believe, are blessed (v. 29). What
do you think he meant? In what ways do you think we are blessed
despite not having seen Jesus physically?

....

*Reflect on and pray about your inclination towards faith and/or
doubt and towards scepticism and/or cynicism.*

JEAN W

Man of action and integrity: James

Show me your faith without deeds, and I will show you my faith by what I do.

The writer of this book was probably Jesus' brother, who became a Christian when he saw the risen Christ and later became a church leader in Jerusalem. I think this book and its author are often passed over and ignored, even though they have much wisdom and common sense to teach us.

In our first passage, James draws a vivid picture of people who listen to what God says but don't do it. They are like those who look at themselves in a mirror, then go away and forget what they have seen. By contrast, 'those who look intently into the perfect law that gives freedom, and continue in it... they will be blessed in what they do' (1:25).

In the second passage, he satirises those who say the right words but don't take appropriate action. They see someone in need of food and clothing and tell them to go in peace and keep warm and well fed. 'What good is that?' he asks pointedly. For James, faith is a sham unless it's exercised. For him, this a matter of genuineness and integrity. For me—if faith is a gift from God—then it's a gift that needs to be accepted and used or it's useless and a mockery.

I often think of some words of Jesus on this matter: 'Why do you call me, "Lord, Lord," and do not do what I say? (Luke 6:46). 'Not everyone who says to me, "Lord, Lord," will enter the kingdom of heaven, but only those who do the will of my Father who is in heaven' (Matthew 7:21).

....

Do you believe that what we believe and how we behave are inseparable? Reflect, in God's presence, upheld by his love and forgiveness, on the match between your beliefs and your behaviour, your words and your actions.

JEAN W

Loving, imaginative and intuitive: John

Dear friends, let us love one another, for love comes from God. Everyone who loves has been born of God and knows God… God is love.

For the character of John we have a rich treasury to draw from—the Gospels, his three letters and the book of Revelation.

Read through today's passage and you will not be surprised that John was known as the apostle of love. He seems to be overwhelmed by God's love and gently exhorts his 'dear friends' to reflect that love to one another. Furthermore, we are to 'live in love' and hence 'live in God', for 'God is love'. Perfect love—which none of us has attained but which we must all long for—drives out all fear. John adds that anyone who says he loves God and hates his brother or sister in Christ is a liar. Very strong words from this gentle apostle!

I wonder what other characteristics or pictures come to your mind when you think of John? I think of him sitting beside Jesus at the last supper and leaning against him (John 13:25). When Jesus said that someone at the table would betray him, Peter nudged John and asked him to ask Jesus who he meant. Clearly John and Jesus were very close friends. I also think of John beside the cross of Jesus and of Jesus asking John to take care of his mother, in those memorable words, 'Woman, here is your son… Here is your mother' (John 19:26–27). What trust Jesus showed in John's caring character!

It's a surprise, after all, to remember that John and his brother James were described by Jesus earlier as 'sons of thunder' (Mark 3:17), perhaps indicating that they had fiery, volatile aspects to their characters. If so, it seems that John could also be, or had changed into, a calm, caring and loving person. He was also, I believe, a reflective, intuitive and rather poetic and lyrical one, judging by the wonderful first chapter of John and the book of Revelation.

....

Choose a verse or verses about love from today's passage to reflect on and take with you into the day, either as an encouragement or as a way of relating to others.

JEAN W

Elaine Pountney writes:

When I think back to a summer in the Canadian prairies that I spent with my aunt and uncle, and a week-long tent revival meeting, I shudder to remember the old-fashioned 'hellfire and brimstone' preacher. The shouting, arm-flailing man terrified the life out of me! I was nine years old at the time and had nightmares for weeks. I repented day and night, convinced I was doomed to hell.

So how do we read the fiery prophets of old without dismissing them lock, stock and barrel or without becoming overly obsessed with gloom, doom and damnation?

We read the book of Isaiah in the context of the big picture of our world and with the wide lens of the whole Bible. The book of Isaiah is a message to the nation of Israel first and, second, to all the nations surrounding Israel at that time. It is also a prophecy that prepares all nations across the centuries for the coming of Messiah, who will rescue not just individuals, and not just Israel, but all nations from the inevitable chaos created on the international stage. It is also a prophecy that looks ahead to the day when Jesus will reign with righteousness on earth, when the full impact of his death and resurrection take effect in the new heaven and the new earth.

No matter how many generations have received, read and even understood God's words through the prophet Isaiah, God's people are rebellious or indifferent and nations become proud and aggressive. So Isaiah's words are as relevant today as they were in 600BC: they still hold the power and authority of God as he calls us to account today.

There are hard, even severe, words of judgment throughout the prophecy, but look for strong, life-giving words of God's love for his people and his creation, for God's heartbeat of mercy and invitation, and for vibrant hope in the middle of all the global confusion and disaster. We start in the first six chapters with Isaiah's vision—his encounter with holiness, his call 'to go' and his response.

A vision, a message, a messenger

Hear me, you heavens! Listen, earth! For the Lord has spoken: I reared children and brought them up, but they have rebelled against me. The ox knows its master, the donkey its owner's manger, but Israel does not know, my people do not understand.

Recently, my husband and I rewatched the movie about William Wilberforce, *Amazing Grace*. It provoked us. Between 1807 and 1833, Wilberforce showed great passion and determination to pass legislation in the British Parliament that would abolish the slave trade in Britain. His commitment and determination caused me to ask if I cared enough about anything to keep me that passionate about it for so long? God had given Wilberforce a vision—a vision of what could be and should be: dignity and respect for all people and all nations equally. That was the God-given message and Wilberforce was the messenger.

Visions from God are often costly, rarely asked for or even wanted, taking individuals into arenas they would not otherwise enter, exacting boldness from normally benign temperaments and demanding confrontation of culturally passive norms—with no promise that their message will be received.

Isaiah's message from God to his people and to the nations was not popular. Israel's leadership was broken and corrupt and the people were self-serving, empty and rebellious. This was a message for Israel, for those in spiritual and political power in Jerusalem. It was also a message for the kings, rulers and nations surrounding Israel and Judah—just as Wilberforce's vision was for rulers, economic barons and people of many nations.

Visions from God speak into global issues. They are a call to his people and the nations of the world to get back on track, to put things right, to choose justice and mercy, to shake off their diffidence and passive rebellion and return to truth.

....

Creator God, we are so comfortable in our own ways, our indifference and our blindness. Awaken us to see your vision and hear your message for our own nation in these times.

ELAINE P

A prophet: speaking the words of God

Why should you be beaten any more? Why do you persist in rebellion? Your whole head is injured, your whole heart afflicted. From the sole of your foot to the top of your head there is no soundness—only wounds and bruises and open sores, not cleansed or bandaged or soothed with oil.

There were five of us in our small group. We were all at a 'training of facilitators' workshop in Zambia. Each person in the small group was required to facilitate a practice presentation of a key point of the workshop. A tall, stately man from Tanzania got up to present his key points to our small group. He was a quiet man but one who had an unusual dignity and authority. He began his presentation and, within 30 seconds, the four of us who were recipients of his presentation were silenced and in tears. We were captured by the presence that was upon his teaching. His words were not a surprise—we already knew what he was going to say—but there was a profound authority in his words, even in a practice session.

Isaiah was a messenger with that kind of prophetic authority. He was anointed to be God's voice to bring God's words to the people. And the message? Isaiah is to proclaim the charges that God is bringing against the nation of Israel and the nations surrounding Israel and Judah: 'Hear the word of the Lord, you rulers of Sodom; listen to the instruction of our God, you people of Gomorrah' (v. 10).

Whether they like the words or not, or even if they find the prophet a burr under their kingly robes, the kings and rulers stop to listen to the messages he brings, because he speaks with the authority of the Lord Almighty. Who has the authority of the Lord Almighty with our rulers and politicians in the nations of our world today? Who are they willing to listen to? What charges does God bring against our nations today?

....

Send us your prophet to show us the injured head and afflicted heart of our own nations—our own wounds, bruises and open sores—so that we might be healed.

ELAINE P

A charge against the people

Stop doing wrong, learn to do right! Seek justice, encourage the oppressed. Defend the cause of the fatherless, plead the case of the widow… If you are willing and obedient, you will eat the best from the land; but if you resist and rebel, you will be devoured by the sword.

Isaiah's prophetic vision is a strong message of judgment and a passionate plea for the people to return to God. Israel, having received so many privileges from God, is ungrateful and self-serving. Jerusalem, is filled with murderers and thieves, with rulers loving bribes and ignoring the plight of the fatherless and the widow. The people have closed their ears to God's message and shut their eyes against their own corruption. Through his messenger, God brings this charge against his own people: 'You have spurned the Holy One of Israel' (see 1:4).

A man faithfully stands on a busy intersection near our home, holding a big sign: 'Repent! Prepare to meet your Maker!' Some smile tolerantly while mocking him. Some wave and say, 'Good morning'. Some yell unkind words at him.

So what might a prophet of God look like in our cities today? Perhaps a journalist who exposes political corruption. A judge sentencing a religious leader who has been found guilty of the sexual abuse of children. A report exposing government policies that pay handsome salaries to those who are already rich but quash low-cost housing for the elderly. An irritating activist who gathers people to march for the homeless. Are these the Isaiahs and Wilberforces of our times?

It is God who raises up the prophets who call our nations to repent and seek mercy for our selfish and disobedient behaviour, and it is God who speaks strong warnings of the consequences if we stubbornly resist and rebel. 'Come now, let us reason together' is the Lord's invitation. 'Though your sins are like scarlet, they shall be as white as snow; though they are red as crimson, they shall be like wool' (v. 18).

....

Thank you, Holy One, that you continue to extend your invitation and your power to transform even our sins of rebellion and injustice. Thank you that you continue to send us prophets.

ELAINE P

An inevitable consequence

I will sing for the one I love a song about his vineyard… He dug it up and cleared it of stones and planted it with the choicest vines… Then he looked for a crop of good grapes, but it yielded only bad fruit… What more could have been done for my vineyard than I have done for it?

Isaiah 5 starts out with the tenderness of deep love and affection and ends with darkness and distress. What happened to the opening song of love for the plants of his vineyard? I remember, as a teenager, listening to one of the most powerful evangelists I have ever heard. He was gifted—a choice vine. Two decades later, I listened to news stories that announced a litany of sexual exploits, corrupt accounting and misuse of people by the same evangelist. Somewhere, that 'choice vine' had begun to produce only bad fruit.

As Isaiah speaks to these choice vines, he announces a litany of woes to the nation of Israel: 'Woe to you who add house to house' (v. 8); 'Woe to those who… run after their drinks' (v. 11); woe to those who use deceit and so bind themselves to sin (v. 18); woe to those who call evil good and good evil (v. 20); woe to those who think they are so smart (v. 21); woe to those who are champions of the guilty and violate the innocent by taking bribes (v. 23).

God's judgment against the elders and leaders of his people resonates with nations globally: 'It is you who have ruined my vineyard… What do you mean by crushing my people and grinding the faces of the poor?' (3:14–15). Embedded in these prophetic words, though, is a passionate plea coming from the depths of God's love. It is a plea that God's people—from the least important to the most powerful brokers of national influence—will reject their self-centred rebellion. It pleads with them to produce a crop of the good fruit of righteousness and justice: their vines still have that potential.

....

Lord God, Master Gardener, bring health back to our personal and national vines, so that we can once again delight in your song of joy in your vineyards around the world.

ELAINE P

A call to the nation

In the last days… Many peoples will come and say, 'Come, let us go up to the mountain of the Lord, to the house of the God of Jacob. He will teach us his ways, so that we may walk in his paths'…
Come, house of Jacob, let us walk in the light of the Lord.

After the devastating judgment and the wars that are to dismantle their nation, there is a promise of hope in the prophet's words: 'in the last days' things will be different. In those last days (a time yet to come), the Lord will return in peace to settle disputes. The people will beat their swords into ploughshares and their spears into pruning hooks, with no more training for war. Peace will ensure that nations produce food enough for all and the Lord will bring order and justice.

We live in the in-between time, however—between these prophetic words of judgment, in the middle of our present brokenness, waiting for the future hope of 'those days'. So how are we to live?

When we lived in the former Soviet Union, we worked with capable young women and men who were choosing to walk in the light of the Lord. They had been educated and formed in a culture of atheism that mocked religious faith. As they talked about their journey to the light of the Lord, almost all of them spoke of their grandmothers or elderly aunts who had prayed with them, taken them to the Orthodox church and read the Bible to them. At the time, they had dismissed faith and talk of God as silly old wives' tales, but today they honour those grandmothers and aunts who courageously kept faith when their national leaders were committed to extinguishing the light.

How, then, are we to live? Like those grandmothers who held on to faith with courage, boldly teaching it to their grandchildren—until 'the last days' come. Being people of peace, choosing ploughshares and pruning hooks to feed the nations and helping to usher in those radically different last days as people of the light.

....

Father, we have forgotten how to walk in the light as a nation. We have looked for peace and stability in wrong places. Teach us your ways and give us the desire to walk in the light of the Lord.

ELAINE P

God's invitation to an individual

I saw the Lord seated on a throne, high and exalted, and the train of his robe filled the temple… 'Woe to me!' I cried. 'I am ruined! For I am a man of unclean lips, and I live among a people of unclean lips, and my eyes have seen the King, the Lord Almighty.'… Then I heard the voice of the Lord saying, 'Whom shall I send? And who will go for us?' And I said, 'Here am I. Send me!'

It was an amazing concert. The violinist—young, beautiful, gifted—had taken us into a place of profound worship and awe. It was her last concert before she left to work as a Bible translator in a remote area of a distant country. People were asking, was God really calling this gifted young musician to go on such a obscure mission, or was it a misplaced zealousness?

Isaiah's unusual prophetic call comes through a vision of God, surrounded in glory, with seraphs singing of God's holiness and glory in a shaking temple full with smoke. Not surprisingly, Isaiah responds with horror, because holiness exposes sinfulness. The closer we are to God's glory, the closer we are to our awareness of sinfulness. God takes a burning coal, touches Isaiah's mouth and says, 'Your guilt is wiped away. Your mouth is ready for God's message' (see v. 7).

Then the invitation comes: 'Whom shall I send? And who will go for us?' (v. 8). Where did these questions come from? Send where? To whom? To do what? Without any hesitation or questioning, though, Isaiah says, 'Here am I. Send me!' I wonder if Isaiah had any idea what he was getting himself into.

The young, beautiful, gifted musician was sent to a people with a tonal language. Only someone with accurate pitch and an ear to hear minor musical differences would have been able to create an accurate representation of the language of the people to whom she had been sent. The job was a perfect fit for perfect pitch.

....

Holy God, you ask us the same questions you asked Isaiah, because you have fitted us perfectly for what perfectly fits us in your world. Give us confidence that you take away our guilt in preparation to 'go where you send us'.

ELAINE P

A strange message

'Make the heart of this people calloused; make their ears dull and close their eyes. Otherwise they might see with their eyes, hear with their ears, understand with their hearts, and turn and be healed.' Then I said, 'For how long, Lord?'

What a strange message for God's people! 'They're going to hear and not get it, look and not have a clue. Their hearts will be like stone. Otherwise they would be healed and changed.' What kind of message is this? Wouldn't this prophetic word of God simply anger and harden hearts more? Most of us do not take kindly to a message that tells us we're blowing it, that we're all messed up. Besides, we are much too sophisticated to hear this simplistic message, aren't we?

Isaiah has a hard road ahead of him if he faithfully proclaims God's message to his people. It's not a great job description and perhaps brings low job satisfaction. Isaiah's prophetic success will come as he perseveres in delivering this hard message, even when both he and his message are ignored, mocked and shut out.

Not surprisingly, Isaiah asks: 'For how long, Lord?' God's surprising answer is, 'Until the cities are empty, the fields are empty and abandoned, the forests have been chopped to stumps, and the land is utterly forsaken' (see vv. 11–12). This description fits countries today that have empty, bombed-out cities, polluted water systems, torched schools and churches and farm land contaminated with mines, where dynasties of corrupt leaders have invested in the destruction of their own country and their own people.

Then God says, 'Don't despair, Isaiah. One of those stumps in those stump-filled forests carries a holy seed. This devastation will not be the end!' (see v. 13). Once again we find God's message of hope embedded in the description of destruction: there is a holy seed that will grow into a strong saviour from this devastation.

....

God of the prophet Isaiah, 'Create in us a pure heart, and renew a steadfast spirit within us. Do not cast us from your presence or take your Holy Spirit from us. Restore to us the joy of your salvation and grant us a willing spirit, to sustain us' (based on Psalm 51:10–12).

ELAINE P

As part of her ongoing series of devotions from Isaiah, Elaine Pountney writes:

We pick up this next section of Isaiah after chapter 6, where Isaiah finds himself in the presence of the holiness and the glory of Almighty God. In response to God's question, 'Whom shall I send?' Isaiah exclaims, 'Here am I. Send me!' and hits the road running. With his son, he is sent to calm King Ahaz of Judah, who is overwhelmed because the kings in the north are forming alliances with Assyria to overtake Judah and Jerusalem—Ahaz' territory! Assyria is a formidable foe that strikes terror into the hearts of God's people.

It is Isaiah's job to tell the people that Assyria will indeed sweep into their land and be victorious over Judah. Why is God allowing this? Because his people are already divided in a disastrous, power-grabbing civil war. God's people are right to be terrified because they have repeatedly been unfaithful to God, choosing to listen to false prophets and forming alliances with surrounding nations rather than turning to the God of Israel for their strength and deliverance.

Woven through these chapters, where Isaiah outlines the consequences of Israel's unfaithfulness, the crumbling of their fortified cities and devastation to the land, is a blessing on the faithful remnant—people who still trusted in God, who held faith in the God of Israel to rescue them and save them from extinction. These people are not saved from the very real, horrendous consequences of war, but they are the hope of the nation: they are the light in the darkness for both Israel and the surrounding nations.

This is the context of chapters 7—12 in Isaiah and it is into this context that hope is announced: the people walking in darkness will see a great light, for a child will be born, a child who will be their salvation. When their world is bleak and unrelenting, when their leaders have led them into disaster after disaster, hope is promised in a child yet to be born who will be their Saviour and defence. Israel will once again sing to the Lord in joy.

Standing firm in a messy civil war

'Let us invade Judah; let us tear it apart and divide it among ourselves...' Yet this is what the Sovereign Lord says: 'It will not take place, it will not happen... If you do not stand firm in your faith, you will not stand at all.'

Isaiah has accepted his call to be God's spokesperson to God's people, knowing that there are difficult years ahead for them. Their hearts are hard, their ears are plugged shut and their eyes are blind to what is really going on (ch. 6). This is the context at the point where we pick up Isaiah's story in chapter 7.

The people of God find themselves in the intensity of a messy civil war. Three kings have joined forces with the northern part of Israel in a strategic move to attack Jerusalem and the southern part of Israel, Judah. The people of the south are terrified—shaking in their boots. Who wouldn't be? God tells Isaiah to take his son and go to meet with the terrified King Ahaz of the south, to tell him, 'Be careful, keep calm and don't be afraid. Do not lose heart because of these smouldering kings of the north. They are stubs of firewood.' The threat of the northern alliance usurping power is going to come to nothing.

Daily news from the north was sensational hype, exaggerating events and prophesying imminent chaos and disaster. So what were the people in the south to believe in? Isaiah's word or their knowledge of the powers amassing on their northern border? The people were genuinely confused by this painful civil war because of competing alliances with surrounding nations that were a very real threat.

God's word to the people of Judah in Isaiah's time might be just as true for us today: 'If you do not stand firm in your faith, you will not stand at all' (v. 9). Perhaps God is saying the same thing to us today: stand firm in faith. God's people have always been defined by faith: if there is no faith in God, then there are no people of God.

....

Sovereign Lord, are you absent from our world and deaf to the cries of people in war zones? Give us faith to stand when we do not understand the battle.

ELAINE P

Trying the patience of God

Again the Lord spoke to [King] Ahaz, 'Ask the Lord your God for a sign, whether in the deepest depths or in the highest heights.' But Ahaz said, 'I will not ask; I will not put the Lord to the test.'

At first reading, not asking for a sign appears to demonstrate that deep faith in God—but it is God who is inviting Ahaz to ask for a sign. It would have helped Ahaz understand more fully what was happening in Judah and the surrounding nations. In not asking for a sign, he is demonstrating the opposite of faith. Ahaz, king of God's people, did not get it! The future of Israel's royalty was dependent on Ahaz having courage to lead God's people in faith.

Ahaz does not have enough faith to believe that the Lord his God is greater than the nations that scheme against Judah. Exasperated, prophet Isaiah explodes: 'Hear now, you house of David! Is it not enough to try the patience of human beings? Will you try the patience of my God also?' (v. 13). In spite of Ahaz' unbelief, God does give him a sign, a strange sign: a young girl who is still a virgin will bear a son and will name him 'God-is-with-us'. He will grow to be a king who will reject the wrong and choose the right, but, before the coming of that son, a time unlike anything ever known will descend upon God's people. Foreign powers, like flies and bees, will invade, overrun their country and strip it of its beauty and bounty. Their vineyards and farms will turn to weeds and brambles. Foreigners will shave the hair off their heads, their genitals and their men's faces, leaving them shamed and exposed—naked to the nations.

The hope of God's people lies in the royal heir born to a young virgin. Then, God will once more reside with his people, raising up a new people of God who will put their hope in this king called Immanuel, God-with-us.

....

Lord Jesus, Immanuel, as we fear wars, reduce our arable land to concrete and wasteland and push men and women to homelessness, like Ahaz we try your patience. Please turn our eyes to yourself—our only hope.

ELAINE P

Who do we put our hope in?

'Don't be like this people, always afraid somebody is plotting against them. Don't fear what they fear... If you're going to worry, worry about The Holy. Fear God-of-the-Angel-Armies. The Holy can be either a Hiding Place or a Boulder blocking your way.'

As my husband and I sat in the oncologist's office, we were told that a fairly aggressive cancer was present and treatment was to start immediately. That C-word hit like a well-aimed missile in our hearts. We were assured that the multiple treatments would be effective—not to worry (easy words to speak, not so easy to swallow). The treatments were arduous and long but the cancer was contained and eliminated.

The nation of Assyria was Israel's cancer treatment. The Lord had just given King Ahaz a sign of hope, but Israel's national cancer needed radical surgery that would leave deep scars on the land, the people and the royal line. Nations surrounding Israel would mock and toy with Israel as God skilfully used Assyria as the scalpel and radiation treatment to rid Israel of its unfaithfulness to the Holy One.

In desperation, the nation turned to foreign powers to broker peace deals and protection packages—but to no avail. In panic, they turned to fortune tellers for more palatable prophecies than Isaiah was giving them. They went to spiritualists, mediums and the dead for answers. Isaiah said, 'No! Enquire of God instead. Turn back to holy scripture', but Israel tried one thing after another and, when nothing worked, they cursed king and God.

To the small group faithful to God who were swept along in the consequences to the whole nation, Isaiah responds, 'Preserve the teaching for my followers, while I wait for God as long as he remains in hiding... I stand my ground and hope, I and the children God gave me as signs to Israel, warning signs and hope signs from God-of-the-Angel-Armies, who makes his home in Mount Zion' (vv. 16–18).

....

Father, how hard it is when you are silent and we cry out for answers, when we cannot see your big plan for our nations. Help us to say with Isaiah that we stand our ground and hope in you.

ELAINE P

A great light in the shadow of death

The people walking in darkness have seen a great light; on those living in the land of the shadow of death a light has dawned. You have enlarged the nation and increased their joy; they rejoice before you as people rejoice at the harvest... For to us a child is born.

Talking with the parents was confusing. According to them, everything was under control. They could handle what was happening. Their daughter was simply being a typical teenager. But their daughter was out of control, silently crying out for help, on drugs, out all night, drunk and disorderly, her life in chaos.

God's people in Judah are saying the same: 'Things aren't that bad. We can handle anything. If our buildings are knocked down, we'll rebuild them bigger and finer. If our forests are cut down, we'll replant them with finer trees' (v. 10, *THE MESSAGE*). The prophet's words fall on deaf ears. The people are blind to the threats within their nation, continuing to put faith in their own superiority and resiliency.

Isaiah's voice is shouting: 'You don't get it! A time is coming that will be full of distress, chaos and disaster—a time when tribe will turn against tribe within Israel, when surrounding nations will wage war against Israel. A time when your elders and prominent leaders will mislead and your prophets will speak lies. Truth and good leadership will vanish and the nations will flounder.'

But then, after all these calamities have come upon them, a time is coming when 'there will be no more gloom for those who were in distress' (v. 1, NIV). Celebration and joy will fill the land again, for a child will be born from the royal line of kings. This child will rule with justice and goodness, with integrity and right-relatedness, and will put things right. The people will rejoice again. Isaiah implores them, 'Now is the time to return to God. Now is the time to turn away from your indifference, from your independent, rebellious ways.'

....

God, give us courage to look into the eyes of calamity and also ahead to that great light dawning, so that we can hear what you have to say to us.

ELAINE P

Beware what you think and do

Woe to those who make unjust laws, to those who issue oppressive decrees, to deprive the poor of their rights and withhold justice from the oppressed of my people, making widows their prey and robbing the fatherless. What will you do on the day of reckoning, when disaster comes from afar? To whom will you run for help?

Isaiah 10 reads like a fifth-form history book of our world: nations rise in power and prestige and become arrogant, boasting of their own prowess, their superior goals and purposes, only to become obnoxious in their sense of self-importance, with global ambitions to conquer everything. It's much like our current international scene.

The prophet chants the litany of Israel's ungodliness: inept leadership; wilful making of decrees in the interests of class division and personal gain. Administrators take advantage of defenceless widows and homeless children, manipulating justice for financial gain. Are we any better? We have child prostitutes in every major city, widows' pensions being misused by greedy children and corruption in our police forces, governments and economic institutions.

God said, 'Enough! I will use Assyria to discipline and bring my people back to faith and godliness.' But, in arrogance, Assyria thought, 'By the strength of my hand I have done this… I removed the boundaries of nations… I subdued their kings' (v. 13). God responded to Assyria's arrogance, 'Does an axe take over from the one who swings it? Does a saw act more important than the sawyer?… As if a hammer used the carpenter to pound nails!' (v. 15, *THE MESSAGE*).

It was God—not Assyria—who decided what happened to Israel. It is God who determines what happens to nations when they do not stand in faith. It is God who holds his people accountable for what they do. Once again, woven into the text is a message to those who hold faith: one day, the Holy One of Israel will put all this right.

....

Father, how easy it is to think that we—axe, saw or hammer—are independent of or in charge of you, Creator of nations. Discipline us and correct our arrogance.

ELAINE P

New shoot from chopped-off stump

A shoot will come up from the stump of Jesse... The Spirit of the Lord will rest on him—the Spirit of wisdom and of understanding, the Spirit of counsel and of might, the Spirit of knowledge and fear of the Lord—and he will delight in the fear of the Lord.

I began wondering if I would make it to the top. I was hot and aching. We had been climbing for the last four hours through valleys of dense dark forest that rose into steep climbs. Just about the time I thought I could not climb another step, we emerged to the rocky summit. In stunned awe we looked down on the Pacific Ocean currents wrapping around the Gulf Islands at the feet of majestic, snow-covered mountains. It was awesome. Aching pain faded into insignificance.

Leaving the dark valleys and steep inclines of chapter 10, Israel suddenly emerges to catch a glimpse of the full-colour, wide-angle view of the glorious hope of what is to come in chapter 11. It's a mountain-top view. An offshoot from the royal line of King David will rise up—one clothed in the Spirit of the Lord, with wisdom, understanding, counsel and might; one who delights in the fear of the Lord and will administer justice rightly. This king will usher in a new order where wolf and lamb, calf and lion live in harmony; where a defenceless infant is unthreatened by the cobra and the impulsive toddler is safe even when exploring a viper's nest. It's almost unimaginable.

Just as unimaginable is a new world order where all nations will be gathered under the Lord's banner of righteousness and the whole earth 'will be filled with the knowledge of the Lord as the waters cover the sea' (v. 9). What kind of eyes will we need to look at all nations in this way? What kind of heart will we need to stand shoulder-to-shoulder with women and men of all nations—even those nations that have attacked and injured our loved ones? It will take the Spirit of the Lord himself to accomplish this.

....

Lord God, we long for these days on our earth, with a deep yearning for this new world order. Give us this wisdom and understanding in our world.

ELAINE P

Return from exile

In that day you will say: 'I will praise you, Lord. Although you were angry with me, your anger has turned away and you have comforted me. Surely God is my salvation; I will trust and not be afraid.'

Do you remember the pictures of people streaming into the streets of cities across England on the day the Allies declared that World War II was over? They were pictures of people dancing and singing, of strangers hugging and kissing, of laughter and chatter. There were tears of joy on weary faces and relief easing wrinkled brows. In the background were bombed-out buildings, battle debris and a war-weary land. But on that day, there were songs of joy.

Chapter 12 is just such a picture. The horror of the nation-crushing wars that Israel has endured is over. God is bringing back his people from distant exile. God is drawing buckets of living water from the well of salvation to satisfy their thirst. Women and men rise up to testify that God's anger has turned into comfort, that God is their salvation. Trust is back; fear is gone. There is strength in this restored relationship with God and, once again, the people put their faith in God.

In that day, the whole nation, with one voice, is giving thanks to the Lord and calling on his name for what they need (v. 4). Their deep drinks of personal salvation become an unstoppable proclamation of the good things that God has done for them and the wonder of who he is. It is a proclamation to the surrounding nations—even those nations that attacked them. The people's personal experiences of God's good character and his powerful actions erupt into tears of relief, hugs of comfort and songs of joy.

A new order has begun. Post-war, post-exile, post-God's anger, the people of God rise up shouting aloud and singing with joy because the Holy One of Israel is back among them.

....

'Give praise to the Lord, call on his name; make known among the nations what he has done… Sing to the Lord, for he has done glorious things; let this be known to all the world. Shout aloud and sing for joy… for great is the Holy One of Israel among you' (vv. 4–6).

ELAINE P

A warning: Isaiah 13—26 will be hard chapters to read! The prophet's words describe Israel's unfaithfulness to her God and her flirtatious history with the nations surrounding her—and the terrible cost of such choices for the people. The nations surrounding Israel also come under the scrutiny and judgment of God. Isaiah lists them by name, describing each one with its distinctive pride and arrogance, its corruption and its misuse of power, which are ultimately the cause of the demise of each country. History confirms Isaiah's prophetic words. Surprisingly, though, woven into these prophetic words of judgment are threads of hope for the future—insights into God's heart of compassion for all people and each nation.

Although these chapters read like a history lesson, there are critical lessons for us to learn today from the Assyrian and the Babylonian empires, and from Moab and Egypt. They are lessons that will bring faithful believers back into right relationship with God. They will force us out of an individualistic mindset, critical of other nations, into God's international, global perspective. Isaiah understood that Israel was to be a light to the nations: Israel was never intended to keep God to herself. God's goal in revealing himself to the people of this one nation was that, through them, people from every tribe and every nation would be brought to faith in the Almighty God. Being God's people does not bring a presumption of superiority but a mandated responsibility to proclaim God to the nations.

Isaiah turns our vision from the past to a future time: 'in that day' is a phrase we read over and over again. In that day, God will correct injustices and inequities, the faithful remnant will find relief and peace, and the nations will be brought together in unity and worship, in the goodness of the Lord.

The final chapters take us into the centre of the city of Zion, where God reigns with justice, mercy and righteousness. This is a holy city where the faithful remnant are dancing in joy through the streets.

As we look forward through Advent to Christmas, celebrating Christ's coming as a baby, let's look on to that day when he comes again, when we will be with him for ever.

Learning from Babylon and Assyria

How you have fallen from heaven... You have been cast down to
the earth, you who once laid low the nations! You said in your
heart, 'I will ascend to heaven; I will raise my throne above the
stars of God... I will make myself like the Most High.'

Chapters 13—24 of Isaiah are hard to read, with their severe words
describing raw consequences, but there are important things for us
to learn today from each country addressed. Each nation had been
given power and wealth, yet each abandoned and rejected the
source of their power and wealth. Let's take a deep breath and brace
ourselves for the prophet's words.

Isaiah prophesies the end of mighty Assyria and majestic Babylon—unimaginable when both were at the height of their prestige.
Isaiah's challenge is, 'If this prophecy comes true, you must listen
carefully to all these words of God for the days yet to come.' Power,
arrogance and indifference—hallmarks of these empires—crushed
the widows, abused the orphans, ridiculed God's people of faith and
ultimately caused the empires themselves to crumble. Surprisingly,
though, it is their crumbling ruins that will bring faithful people back
to the God of all nations, back to singing praises to the righteous one.

We know that human power and political will can be distorted,
ugly and evil, but we struggle to find God in some of the terrifying
prophecies against the nations in Isaiah. We are forced to step back
and take a long view of these 2500-year-old messages about the will
of God, yet to be completely fulfilled. Because the Assyrian and Babylonian empires did end in desolation, we are drawn to listen again
to all the words of the prophet for a time yet to come—a time for us.
Even today, the Lord continues to demonstrate both his hand of judgment and his hand of compassion as he binds faithful believers from
Israel and from other nations together as his new people.

....

*Righteous one, unless you give us eyes to see the long view, we will
not be able to hear and understand the words of the prophet. Give
us gifts of insight and wisdom as we read these difficult chapters of
Isaiah.*

ELAINE P

Learning from Moab

We have heard of Moab's pride... but her boasts are empty...
My heart laments for Moab like a harp, my inmost being for Kir
Hareseth. When Moab appears at her high place, she only wears
herself out; when she goes to her shrine to pray, it is to no avail.

My mind is strangely uncomfortable as I sit here trying to write a
suitable note from today's reading. My mind is full of questions and
emotions because I remember listening to a mum weeping in agony.
Her daughter had just died from a bad batch of street drugs: 'She was
smart, intelligent, in control—she thought she could handle it!' Her
daughter had been beautiful, gifted, moving with the 'in-crowd', loving the glamour and glitz of it all. She'd had it all!

The nation of Moab also loved the glamour and glitz of its beauty
and thought its status could easily be maintained through clever nego-
tiations. The prophet's words of judgment, though wrapped in poetic
language, are a strong rebuke from God with clear consequences.

Equally loud and clear is God's grief over Moab: 'The waters of
Nimrim are dried up and the grass is withered; the vegetation is gone
and nothing green is left' (15:6); the choicest vines are trampled and
the women are left vulnerable. God has been unable to draw this
nation to truth and faithfulness, but still his heart beats passionately
for it: 'My heart laments for Moab like a harp, my inmost being for Kir
Hareseth' (16:11). The Lord is not a distant spectator of the world's
sorrow but one who identifies with lament, all the while knowing
that it is his own hand of severe mercy that is causing such agony.

Moab's envoys, pleading for asylum, cannot save—help will not
come from the surrounding nations—but there is hope. There are no
promises of release from the consequences of their choices, but God
will not forget the Moabites. Their time of discipline will end, just as
assuredly as a contract binds a servant for a limited time (16:14).

....

Spirit of God, guard our hearts and minds from pride and conceit,
personally and nationally. Let us wrestle with your hard words to
Moab so that we will learn well what Moab has to teach us today.

ELAINE P

Learning from Damascus

You have forgotten God your Saviour; you have not remembered the Rock, your fortress... Although the peoples roar like the roar of surging waters, when he rebukes them they flee far away, driven before the wind like chaff on the hills, like tumbleweed before a gale.

It was an alliance that doomed two nations to God's judgment. Ephraim, one of the northern tribes of Israel, turned to Damascus seeking a secure alliance against the advancing armies of Assyria; Damascus sought divine help from God's people in the north. But unfaithful Israel could not be made secure by a worldly power, and Damascus could not be made secure by turning to Israel, because Israel had abandoned her God and was unable to extend God's blessing, even by association, to any other country.

It reminds us of the classic movie theme in which a clever, ambitious but poor and socially unacceptable young man woos a beautiful, socially elite and wealthy young woman into marriage—only to discover that, upon marriage, the woman is cut off from the family wealth because of her choice of husband. We then find that the ambitious young man never really loved his bride anyway.

The prophet exposes the consequence of this futile romance between northern Israel and Damascus. 'In that day', the glory of God's people will fade and the people will waste away. Their fortified cities will be taken over by brambles and thickets, suffocating the finest imported plants that they themselves have planted and tended.

The nations rage like the boiling waters of a raging sea, but, at the sound of the Lord's commanding rebuke, the surrounding nations are silent—blown away as if they were nothing but dandelion fluff (v. 13). In that authoritative quietness, there is hope. A remnant of faithful believers will stand—and this remnant will look no longer to man-made gods but, once again, to their Creator, the Holy One of Israel.

Holy one, it is so tempting to look to others for help rather than to you. Today, by the power of your word, blow away what is not of you and what will not last.

See what James has to say about waves and wind in 1:6–8.

ELAINE P

Learning from the Egyptians

When [the Egyptians] cry out to the Lord because of their oppressors, he will send them a saviour and defender, and he will rescue them. So the Lord will make himself known to the Egyptians, and in that day they will acknowledge the Lord.

Like the Assyrian and Babylonian empires, Egypt had a glorious history. Egypt was the first and most clearly remembered adversary of God's people; yet in this chapter we read that 'in that day' the Egyptians, alongside Israel, will be blessed and will be a blessing on the earth.

Before that day, though, God has much to say about Egypt. The Lord rides in on a swift cloud, causing the Egyptian gods to tremble and be useless and the people to lose heart. Brother will fight brother; city will fight city; other foreigners hostile to the Egyptians will fight and win. Chaos and disunity will descend on the land, humiliation and defeat on the people. Even the land will withdraw its fruitfulness and the Nile will dry up. Egypt will stagger in bewilderment, not knowing which way to turn, hopeless and helpless.

Then the Lord will intervene, preparing Egypt for the blessing that will come. 'In that day' they will fear the Lord—the beginning of wisdom for the Egyptians; in that day Egypt will swear allegiance to the Lord; they will cry out to the Lord and he will be their saviour and rescuer; Egypt, Assyria and Israel will worship the Lord together and will be mutually blessed. The Lord will pronounce, 'Blessed be Egypt my people, Assyria my handiwork, and Israel my inheritance' (v. 25). This is mind-boggling! Think of nations at war with one another in our own time, each desiring to obliterate the other, and imagine them coming together as one in reconciliation, worshipping Almighty God.

Before that day, Egypt will have a painful journey through intense humiliation, defeat and chaos within her land and among her people, until she cries out to the Lord, repents and turns to him in worship.

....

Father, it is very hard to accept the necessity of your discipline to bring whole nations to their knees. Help us see your hand of discipline in our own world, our own nation and our own time, through the eyes of these prophetic words for Egypt.

ELAINE P

119

A history lesson from the Lord

Earth is polluted by its very own people, who have broken its laws, disrupted its order, violated the sacred and eternal covenant. Therefore a curse, like a cancer, ravages the earth… But there are some who will break into glad song… From the four winds and the seven seas we hear the singing: 'All praise to the Righteous One!'

As if we're not disheartened enough by all the prophecies against world nations, chapter 24 hits us with another blow of cosmic proportions! So hang on to your hats while you read this chapter—and look for the glimmer of hope woven into the description of our world.

God takes full responsibility: it is he who lays waste the earth (v. 1). All are impacted equally—priest and lay people, owners and workers, bankers and beggars. Why? Because the people of the world have polluted it. There is no more wine and no more songs or singers. Chaotic cities are uninhabitable: anarchy reigns and people riot in the streets for wine. The cities are deserted, bulldozed into piles of rubble. Terror reigns: pits and booby traps are everywhere. Earth is wobbling out of control, collapsing under the weight of its piled-up sins.

In the middle of all this, a song will rise from the ends of the earth, shouting of God's majesty, broadcasting God's fame; and from the four winds and the seven seas a song rises: 'All praise to the Righteous One!' The last half of the last verse announces that 'in that day' the Lord Almighty will reign from Mount Zion and Jerusalem, splendid and glorious before all his leaders. Whew! That is a great relief. Without this hope of the Lord's rule, how will any of us survive the in-between time of devastation as universal laws are broken, creation order is disrupted and the sacred, eternal covenant is violated?

So we all wait, watching our earth convulsing through war and pollution and violence. A new heaven and a new earth, with a rule of righteousness, is coming (2 Peter 3:13).

....

Father, this chapter is a blaring wake-up call to keep your laws, honour your creation order and keep your covenant. Strengthen us to do it.

Revelation 21:1–5 gives us some insight into the new heaven and new earth that are coming.

ELAINE P

Learning joy in the Lord

He will swallow up death for ever. The Sovereign Lord will wipe away the tears from all faces... In that day they will say, 'Surely this is our God; we trusted in him, and he saved us... let us rejoice and be glad in his salvation.'

As each successive wave slammed their 40-foot sailboat into the rocky outcrop, my daughter and three other sailors began throwing survival equipment on to the exposed rocks of the reef—radio first, sleeping bags next, themselves last. All had leapt to safety in time to watch their boat disintegrate and disappear into the Pacific Ocean. After what seemed like an eternity in the darkness of night, the coast-guard arrived, throwing survival suits and lifelines to them. To be alive was a miracle and their hot-chocolate celebration reflected that.

'In that day' when the Lord Almighty will reign on Mount Zion, women and men from every nation will raise their voices as one, in praise of the marvellous things God has done. God has rescued them from the devastation that we have been reading about and there is great joy being celebrated in the city of Zion. They are safe in the city of God under the protective care of the holy one.

The nations of the world are gathering in Zion, rejoicing that they have been rescued. They have survived the devastation of their lands, and they know that it is the Lord Almighty who has saved their lives. Fortified cities are in ruin, strongholds are broken down, but the city of God has become 'a refuge for the poor, refuge for the needy in their distress, a shelter from the storm' (v. 4).

On this holy Mount Zion, God will 'destroy the shroud that enfolds all peoples... he will swallow up death for ever' (vv. 7–8). Hooray! God will silence the song of the ruthless, at last; and a feast, an extravagant banquet, is being prepared for a festive celebration, the likes of which we have never experienced.

....

God of all nations, hold this prophetic picture of praise and celebration firm in our minds; release our mouths to praise your perfect faithfulness, for you have done marvellous things, things planned long ago.

ELAINE P

Learning to wait in hope

The path of the righteous is level; you, the Upright One, make the way of the righteous smooth. Yes, Lord, walking in the way of your laws, we wait for you... My soul yearns for you in the night; in the morning my spirit longs for you.

As a teenager I watched with fascination as the Civil Rights movement gathered momentum in the summer of 1963. Over 200,000 people gathered on the streets of Washington DC to join a march advocating racial harmony and equality and listened to Martin Luther King's soul-stirring vision: 'I have a dream.' Black Americans had waited in hope for this moment of visibility for a long time.

The people of God also wait in hope for 'that day' when they will sing of freedom in the city of God. They wait for the day when the high and mighty will be brought low and the cities of oppression will be reduced to dust, when the poor will reclaim land that is rightfully theirs—the day when the gates will be flung open for women and men of faith from every nation to find peace, when their paths will be smooth and level. Even then, 'in that day', the wicked will still not choose right living; their blindness will be unchanged. Even then they will show contempt for God's glory and spit on the Lord's majesty.

With the prophet (v. 9), our soul yearns for the God of our salvation through our night, and in our morning our spirit longs for the holy city to welcome us—waiting as a woman about to give birth cries out in pain. The instruction to God's people 'in that day' is to go home, shut their doors and hide until God's judgment passes, until the Lord comes to find them and welcome them into his holy city.

Prophet Isaiah weaves strong colours of hope and expectation into a picture of dark despair. He calls us to 'trust in the Lord for ever, for the Lord, the Lord, is the Rock eternal' (v. 4). He is the Rock for all people, for all times.

....

Thank you, Upright One, that one day you will make all things right.
Open our hearts to live in hope so that we can live rightly in faith.

ELAINE P

Elaine Pountney, who is leading us through this series of devotions on Isaiah, warned us that chapters 13—26 would be hard to read. The season of Advent highlights the contrast between the darkness of our sinful world and the light that Christ brings. Sometimes the darkness seems to overwhelm us. It seems as if there is no hope. But it is often at those darkest times when God is doing his deepest and most significant work: it takes time to refine gold or cut a precious gem to bring out its beauty.

I (Catherine Butcher) wrote these Advent notes at the end of two of the toughest years I have known. Writing these 14 studies was a lifeline, reminding me that God consistently breaks into difficult situations when hope seems to be gone, bringing light and hope. As I wrote, I was hanging on to that promise in Jeremiah 29:11: '"For I know the plans I have for you," declares the Lord, "plans to prosper you and not to harm you, plans to give you hope and a future."'

Three months on, as I add this link page, circumstances have been transformed. The prayers of the twelve friends and family members who stood with me through the darkest days have been answered.

I trust that, as you use these devotional notes in the last two weeks of this year, you will be encouraged by these Bible characters who dared to hope when all hope seemed to be gone. From the darkness of Eden, when sin entered the world, separating humanity from God's presence, through to the first Pentecost and the coming of God's promised Holy Spirit—God is in the business of bringing resurrection hope into our world.

Each day's devotion ends with a short extract from one of the great hymns that are often sung in Advent. As you read the Bible passage for the day and consider how God brings hope to banish our hopelessness, allow the words of the song to sink in so that you carry the message of hope with you throughout the day, with the song singing in your spirit. (If you don't know the tune and have access to a computer, visit www.nethymnal.org, type in a line from the hymn, and you can hear the tune as well as reading the whole lyric.)

Darkness and light

The light shines in the darkness, and the darkness has not overcome it.

The drama of the Genesis story begins with darkness. Then God breaks in, bringing light, creativity, love and hope. A perfect home; a happy couple; everything they could wish for in abundance. No need for backbreaking work, just good stewardship of what they have been given by a loving and generous father who delights to spend time with them, walking and talking in the cool of the evening.

It might have been 'happy ever after', but the woman sees something they haven't got. The dream turns sour as they grasp for more and darkness overwhelms them, but God does not give up on them. He clothes them and covers their shame—and, for all people, for all time, he begins a rescue plan so that all sin can be covered. We are part of that great drama, looking for light in the darkness. As Isaiah said, 'The people walking in darkness have seen a great light' (9:2). All of history focuses on Jesus, the one who rescues us, whose death and resurrection set us free and bring us eternal hope.

This year we have been celebrating the 400th anniversary of the publication of the King James Version of the Bible. The Biblefresh initiative has invited people to describe in eight words how the Bible has changed their world and to be pictured holding their life-changing message. Former heroin addict Mandy Ogumokun was pictured standing outside the prison where she was once an inmate: 'Now I am addicted to God,' she wrote. Lord Michael Bates, a Conservative Life Peer, was pictured in a more stately setting. His placard read, 'Now I have a purpose to serve.'

Reading the Bible certainly changes lives, but it is meeting Jesus through the Bible that has the eternal impact. His rescue plan, running through history, recounted in scripture, is our advent hope.

....

O loving wisdom of our God, when all was sin and shame, a second Adam to the fight and to the rescue came.
JOHN NEWMAN (1801–90)

CATHERINE B

Noah: shut in by God

Noah did all that the Lord commanded him... The animals going in were male and female of every living thing, as God had commanded Noah. Then the Lord shut him in.

Sometimes it seems as if all hope is gone. As Noah looked at the sinful state of the people around him, did he wonder how he could bring up godly children surrounded by such violence and corruption? Do you wonder how the church or your extended family can live faithful lives in a society steeped in materialism and secularism?

Noah's solution was to trust God and obey him, no matter how bizarre God's guidance seemed to be and no matter how much he was ridiculed. To follow Noah's lead, we too need to learn to listen, to hear God's voice, to trust him and to act—even when our actions will cut across cultural norms.

History is full of people who have made a difference, hoping against all hope. Wilberforce battled against powerful opponents with a vested interest in the slave trade; Mother Teresa brought comfort to India's poorest people, even though they were close to death; Alexander Solzhenitsyn, who exposed Stalin's prison system in his novels and spent 20 years in exile, was equally outspoken against Western culture, in which people pursue materialism and forget God.

Just as God shut Noah and his family in the ark, we look to him to surround and protect us and those closest to us in the storms of life. Our efforts at self-preservation are not enough. God has not changed from the God of the Old Testament who brought judgment, but his love and grace to us through Jesus mean that there is an alternative. Ask God to surround you with his protecting love, and look forward with hope to his second coming, when his rescue plan will be complete.

....

No ear may hear his coming, but in this world of sin, where meek souls will receive him, still the dear Christ enters in.
PHILLIPS BROOKS (1835–93)

CATHERINE B

Abram: an impossible dream

The Lord had said to Abram, '… All peoples on earth will be blessed through you.' … Abram believed the Lord, and he credited it to him as righteousness.

Abram's story starts with a promise that gives him hope for the future. As the years passed, Abram must have questioned whether or not God had ever really spoken to him. Was he pursuing an impossible dream? To what extent was he to rely on God? Was he to be the master of his own destiny in making the dream a reality? He believed God, but, as the story unfolds, we see Abram taking matters into his own hands. He and his wife found it almost impossible to believe that God would intervene supernaturally—and all hope must have gone before, at the age of 100, he finally became a father.

The Bible seems to be full of stories in which human hopes are finally dashed before God intervenes supernaturally. Noah's family were the only ones left in the world, with no sign of dry land. Abram and Sarah were far too old to become parents. As we will see as we approach Christmas Day, this pattern is repeated in the lives of many biblical heroes.

What about you? Do you have God-given dreams that seem to be impossible? Do you realise that you are part of the fulfilment of the promise that God gave to Abram: 'All peoples on earth will be blessed through you'? God intends to bless you and make you a blessing to others. What does that mean for you today as you prepare for Christmas, as the people around you are getting busier and perhaps more stressed, and as many face loneliness or the sadness of remembered loss at Christmas time?

Ask God to show you today how you can bring fresh hope to others—how you can be a blessing to all those whose lives touch yours.

....

His Name shall be the Prince of Peace, Forevermore adored, The Wonderful, the Counsellor, The great and mighty Lord.
JOHN MORRISON (1746–98)

CATHERINE B

Joseph: a dangerous dreamer

Joseph said to them, '… You intended to harm me, but God intended it for good to accomplish what is now being done, the saving of many lives.'

When Joseph was sold into slavery by his brothers, his dreams came crashing down around him. He'd dreamed that his brothers would bow down to him. Instead they had tried to kill him. Then again in Egypt, when his life had taken a turn for the better and he had become a trusted servant in Potiphar's home, he had been wrongly accused and thrown into prison. During those years in prison he must have been tempted to become as dejected as his fellow prisoners (Genesis 40:6). Instead he went on serving diligently and was given a position of responsibility in the prison. He also went on listening to God. He could have hardened his heart, refusing to be open to God because his hopes had been dashed. He could have become bitter. When his dream finally came true, though, Joseph was still soft-hearted and willing to forgive.

Many years later, another Joseph had high hopes of life with his young bride, Mary. He must have thought she was so pure, so lovely. Instead, he found that she was pregnant and he wasn't the father; he was ready to divorce her (Matthew 1:19). Yet he was willing to turn his life around and believe the impossible when God intervened: 'An angel of the Lord appeared to him… and said, "Joseph… do not be afraid to take Mary home as your wife, because what is conceived in her is from the Holy Spirit. She will give birth to a son, and you are to give him the name Jesus, because he will save his people from their sins"' (Matthew 1:20–21). Joseph did what the angel told him.

Ask God to give you ears that listen to his voice, a pure heart to respond with love and a willing spirit to obey him, whatever he asks you to do.

O holy Child of Bethlehem, descend to us, we pray; cast out our sin and enter in, be born in us today.
PHILLIPS BROOKS (1835–93)

CATHERINE B

Moses: a reluctant redeemer

The Lord said, 'I have indeed seen the misery of my people in Egypt. I have heard them crying out because of their slave drivers, and I am concerned about their suffering. So I have come down to rescue them... So now, go. I am sending you to Pharaoh.'

When Moses saw the oppression of the Hebrew people, he was angry—angry enough to kill an Egyptian. He had been brought up as an adopted son of Pharaoh's daughter, so, humanly speaking, he would have seemed well placed to make a significant difference. But the murder became known and he had to escape, in fear for his life. Decades later, Moses still did not feel able to accept God's call to return to Egypt to play his part in setting the people free from slavery.

Eventually, though, he did go back, with God's promises and demonstrations of power giving him hope: 'I will be with you' (3:12); 'I will stretch out my hand and strike the Egyptians with all the wonders that I will perform among them' (v. 20); 'I will make the Egyptians favourably disposed toward this people, so that when you leave you will not go empty-handed' (v. 21). God gave him the ultimate hope: 'I have promised to bring you up out of your misery in Egypt into the land of the Canaanites... a land flowing with milk and honey' (v. 17).

Centuries later, God's people were under the tyranny of Roman rule, waiting for their Messiah to come to set them free. How many remembered Micah's words: 'But you, Bethlehem Ephrathah... out of you will come for me one who will be ruler over Israel' (5:2)? Were there shepherds in those Bethlehem fields who looked back to Moses' story of release and longed for Micah's prophecy to be fulfilled?

Now that Jesus has returned to his Father, promising to prepare a place for us (John 14:1–3), are we looking for him in every situation to act with his transforming power and love? As children adopted into God's family, we wait with hopeful hearts.

....

O come, O come, Emmanuel! Redeem thy captive Israel, that into exile drear is gone, far from the face of God's dear Son. Rejoice! Rejoice! Emmanuel shall come to thee, O Israel.

TWELFTH CENTURY, TRANS. JOHN M. NEALE (1818–66)

CATHERINE B

Ruth: hope restored

Then the women said to Naomi, 'Blessed be the Lord, who has not left you this day without a redeemer, and may his name be renowned in Israel! He shall be to you a restorer of life and a nourisher of your old age.'

Ruth's situation looked hopeless: widowed while still a childless young woman; living as a poverty-stricken foreigner with her mother-in-law in a strange country and forced to forage for food. Bethlehem, her new home, must have seemed a barren place in every way, yet God provided food, a husband and a son.

Ruth found her kinsman-redeemer—the family member who was required under Israeli custom and law to find someone to marry her or to marry her himself. Without a husband, women in Ruth's situation faced a bleak, hopeless and hungry life.

When Ruth obeys Naomi's instructions and lies at Boaz's feet, saying, 'Spread your wings over your servant, for you are a redeemer' (3:9), her words echo down to us through centuries as we ask our Redeemer, Jesus, to cover us with his robes of righteousness. In Christ, God has provided us with everything we need for an eternal relationship with him, our heavenly Father. His love is practical: Jesus encourages us to ask our Father in heaven even for the basics of daily bread.

At this time of year, when the West seems so focused on shopping as the only preparation needed for Christmas, take time out today to thank God for all he has given you. Thank him for providing a redeemer, Jesus, and look for opportunities to share the hope you have with those you meet who see through the meaninglessness of materialism and long for a more substantial hope. May your life be a means by which others find the gift of new life this Christmas.

....

Come, Thou long expected Jesus, born to set Thy people free; from our fears and sins release us, let us find our rest in Thee.
CHARLES WESLEY (1707–88)

CATHERINE B

Mary: shock and awe

[Elizabeth said] 'Blessed is she who has believed that what the Lord has said to her will be accomplished!'

Zechariah had asked God for a child but had given up hope of that prayer being answered. He even dared to doubt the angel's announcement that he was to be a father. Gabriel's response seems indignant when Zechariah doesn't believe him: 'I am Gabriel. I stand in the presence of God, and I have been sent to speak to you' (v. 19).

Mary also questions the angelic announcement of her impending pregnancy and she receives some explanation—with the encouragement that her cousin Elizabeth has also conceived against all hope. Mary accepts her new situation obediently, but hurries to see Elizabeth, no doubt to check that her own angelic revelation is true. We all need to look for confirmation of God's word to us, especially when it heralds significant changes. Hearing Elizabeth's greeting gives her confirmation: 'Blessed are you among women, and blessed is the child you will bear!' (v. 42).

Childlessness brought disgrace in Elizabeth's time, and to be pregnant without being married could have led to Mary being stoned. Even if they remembered the Old Testament prophecies concerning the Messiah, no one would have imagined that this shameful pregnancy would be the fulfilment of all the hopes of centuries. God seems to delight in doing the impossible in unimaginable ways.

Do you face impossible situations at home, at work, through illness or other difficult circumstances? We don't always know what God is doing in our lives but he can be trusted to work in every situation to bring blessing. This is our hope: 'And we know that in all things God works for the good of those who love him, who have been called according to his purpose' (Romans 8:28).

....

Child in the manger, Infant of Mary, Outcast and Stranger, Lord of all,
Child who inherits all our transgressions, all our demerits on him fall.
Mary M. Macdonald (1789–1872)

CATHERINE B

Jesus: our hope

The angel said to them, '... Today in the town of David a Saviour has been born to you; he is the Messiah, the Lord...' ... All who heard it were amazed at what the shepherds said to them. But Mary treasured up all these things and pondered them in her heart.

Pregnancy is a rollercoaster ride at the best of times. A first pregnancy for a teenager—as Mary probably was—would have been frightening enough, without the added pressure of an angelic announcement, a disappointed fiancé and an exhausting journey away from home just when the baby was due. She must have felt very lonely.

To cap it all, there was nowhere to stay when the baby arrived and she had to make his bed in an animals' feeding trough. Then, just as she was adjusting to the situation, the local shepherds arrived with a strange tale of angels. Mary had a lot to ponder—even more so when wise men arrived to pay homage to her newborn son with exotic gifts that spoke of kingship, priesthood and death (Matthew 2:11).

As she held her baby in her arms, did she feel held in God's loving embrace? Feeding him, changing him and providing for all his physical needs, did she ponder how the Messiah could allow himself to become so vulnerable and dependent? How could God restrict himself to such an extent, taking on all the limitations we face as human beings with all our inadequacies, and why?

Mary's story is unique, but we are all called to trust God in our daily circumstances. Having adequate food, clothes, health care and housing dulls our sense of reliance on God in the West, but God is still the one who supplies all our needs and deserves the response of grateful hearts. As you celebrate Christ's birth today, thank him for the gift of life and for all the blessings that he showers on you each day. Join with the angels in praising God for Jesus—our rescuer, our sustainer and our eternal hope.

....

Hark! The herald angels sing, 'Glory to the newborn King; peace on earth, and mercy mild, God and sinners reconciled!'
CHARLES WESLEY (1707–88)

CATHERINE B

Lamb of God: perfect sacrifice

Abraham answered, 'God himself will provide the lamb.'

Bethlehem is about five miles from Jerusalem. First-century shepherds in that area would always be on the lookout for perfect, blemish-free lambs. Under Jewish law, two one-year-old lambs were sacrificed each day in the temple in Jerusalem (Exodus 29:38), so providing lambs for sacrifice to atone for sins was big business.

The shepherds would have known the story of Abraham and Isaac—the planned sacrifice of Abraham's only son and the 'scape-goat' that God provided in his place. Each year, they would have re-enacted the Passover story with their families, remembering how the blood of a lamb on their doorposts caused the angel of death to pass over the Hebrew families enslaved in Egypt, allowing their firstborn sons to live while the Egyptians' sons died (Exodus 12). They would have known the words of the prophet Isaiah, pointing to a lamb led to slaughter (Isaiah 53) who would 'bear the sin of many' (v. 12).

It is very unlikely, though, that these shepherds would have pieced together the significance of the newborn baby they were seeing: God providing the perfect lamb as a once-for-all sacrifice, whose blood covers our sin and overcomes sin and death, giving us eternal life.

Years later, the writer to the Hebrews drew together the Old Testament pictures and showed how Jesus fleshed them out. The temple and its sacrifices were only a foreshadowing of Christ's role as high priest and also as the perfect sacrifice: 'He entered the Most Holy Place once for all by his own blood, having obtained eternal redemption' (Hebrews 9:12). Marvel with the shepherds and angels today at how God has made it possible for you to have an eternal relationship with him. Read 1 Peter 1:18–20 and worship Jesus, the one who gives us hope, who was 'chosen before the creation of the world, but was revealed in these last times for your sake'.

....

Mild he lays his glory by, born that man no more may die. Born to raise the sons of earth, born to give them second birth.
CHARLES WESLEY (1707–88)

                                                       CATHERINE B

Wise men: filled with wonder

On coming to the house, they saw the child with his mother Mary, and they bowed down and worshipped him. Then they... presented him with gifts of gold and of incense and of myrrh.

Just as God announced Jesus' birth to his people, the Jews, he led Gentiles to witness the birth. The magi studied prophecy and were also on the lookout for astronomical signs to which they attached significance. God spoke to them in the language of the stars that they were seeking to interpret.

God promises, 'You will... find me when you seek me with all your heart' (Jeremiah 29:13–14). The fact that they were prepared to travel long distances in search of revelation from God suggests that the magi were wholehearted. God knows the secret longings of our hearts and responds. Their gifts—gold for a king, frankincense for a priest and myrrh for burial—point to Jesus' purpose: he is King of kings, our great high priest and the sacrificial lamb whose death gives us life.

Many people have been celebrating Christmas this year without any understanding of the one whose birth they are celebrating. Many are seeking spiritual truth: some look to astrology for answers; others perform religious rituals, following laws without discovering God's grace. All need to meet Jesus. Just like the magi, we need an encounter with God-made-flesh, who gives hope and direction to our lives.

You might be the means by which some people will find the answers to their searching. Are you willing to be used by God to help others find him? Most people become Christians through friendship with a Christian; you might be that friend. You don't need a theology degree to share the hope that you have with another person. As Peter said, 'Always be prepared to give an answer to everyone who asks you to give the reason for the hope that you have'. (1 Peter 3:15). Just use your own words, backed with loving action.

....

As with gladness men of old did the guiding star behold; as with joy they hailed its light, leading onward, beaming bright; so, most glorious Lord, may we evermore be led to thee.

WILLIAM CHATTERTON DIX (1837–98)

CATHERINE B

Simeon and Anna: joyful pensioners

'For my eyes have seen your salvation, which you have prepared in the sight of all people, a light for revelation to the Gentiles and for glory to your people Israel.'

The Holy Spirit revealed to Simeon that he would not die before he had seen the Messiah. He was an old man, but he had not hardened his heart or given up hope. He was devout, taking part in worship regularly and learning from scripture, but he didn't rely on others to tell him what God was saying. He listened to God for himself.

Do you long to hear God speak like Simeon did? Age or gender do not qualify or disqualify us from hearing from God. God has said through the prophet Joel, 'I will pour out my Spirit on all people. Your sons and daughters will prophesy, your old men will dream dreams, your young men will see visions. Even on my servants, both men and women, I will pour out my Spirit in those days' (Joel 2:28–29).

As you approach the end of the year, look back on what God seems to have been saying to you this year, or further back to times when you had a strong sense of his calling or assurance. Ask God to speak to you afresh in the coming year, giving you new hope for the future. Prepare your heart to respond to him. Sometimes he speaks through the Bible: by reading his word day by day, you are already opening your heart to hear his words. Sometimes he speaks through a sermon: by taking part in worship with others week by week, you are putting yourself in a place to hear God's voice. But he can also speak in different, sometimes unexpected ways.

Simeon was called to bear witness to the Messiah; that was this pensioner's task. At whatever stage or age you are, ask God to give you a task for 2012—something only you can do, whether that is loving and serving an awkward neighbour or joining a mission project to bear witness to Jesus in another culture.

....

Born thy people to deliver, born a child and yet a King, born to reign in us forever, now thy gracious kingdom bring.

CHARLES WESLEY (1707–88)

CATHERINE B

John: a lone voice

A voice of one calling: 'In the desert prepare the way for the Lord... And the glory of the Lord will be revealed, and all people will see it together.'

Zechariah, John's father, had been told that John would be a prophet 'in the spirit and power of Elijah... to make ready a people prepared for the Lord' (Luke 1:17). With hindsight we can see that John was the one Isaiah had anticipated.

For Elizabeth and Zechariah, though, John must have seemed simply like a difficult teenager. What parent wants their son to spend his time in inhospitable places wearing strange clothes, attracting undesirable followers to join his gang? How many parents try to force their children to conform, rather than loving and accepting them as they struggle to find their own identity and role in the world? How many church congregations criticise young people, failing to give them a welcoming, safe place to flourish through the experimental stage of growing up? Many a young person has rebelled in such circumstances and churches are poorer as a result. I wonder if Zechariah lived to remember Gabriel's words when he read Isaiah's prophecy and watched his son growing up to act very differently from his peers.

Today, as you read Isaiah's prophecy, use its words to pray for parents, especially parents involved in church leadership, who have just come though one of the busiest months in church life. Pray to our heavenly Father who 'gives strength to the weary and increases the power of the weak' (v. 29). As Christmas can bring out the tensions of family life, particularly when small children are fractious and distant relatives are spending time together over the festive period, pray also for the families known to you, thanking God who 'gently leads those that have young' (v. 11), asking that the next generation might welcome Jesus into their lives, finding hope in him.

....

On Jordan's bank the Baptist's cry announces that the Lord is nigh; come, then, and hearken, for he brings glad tidings from the King of kings!

CHARLES COFFIN (1676–1749)

CATHERINE B

Jesus: prophecy fulfilled

'The Spirit of the Lord is on me, because he has anointed me to preach good news to the poor. He has sent me to proclaim freedom.'

In the film *Braveheart*, William Wallace's stirring speech speaks of freedom: he challenges the Scottish army to fight rather than going back to comfortable but captive lives, living out their days in regret. Wallace dies with the word 'freedom' on his lips. It's a theme that resonates from Eden, where a bid for freedom ended in captivity to sin and death. The cry for freedom resonates throughout history, from Hebrew slaves in Egypt, from African slaves in America and from children enslaved by poverty around the world today.

Often, though, our captivity is more subtle. We are imprisoned by fear of what others might think. We are blinded by material wealth that hides our spiritual poverty. We are oppressed, pressed into a mould made by our culture that prescribes how we should live.

Jesus announces freedom and hope for the future: his love banishes fear; he accepts us as we are. He promises to provide for all our needs: 'Bring the whole tithe into the storehouse... See if I will not... pour out so much blessing that you will not have room enough for it' (Malachi 3:10). He wants us to rely completely on him.

He also sets us free from the expectations of others, to serve only him. He even sets us free from religious expectations, religious rituals and religious laws—so much so that Paul had to remind the Galatians, 'Do not use your freedom to indulge the sinful nature' (5:13).

As the year draws to a close, reflect on areas of your life where you have surrendered the freedom that Jesus has won for you. Ask for God's forgiveness and proclaim his freedom. You might want to ask a friend to pray with you, taking to heart Jesus' words in today's reading and in Matthew 18:18–19. Determine to live a life of freedom.

....

Shout, while ye journey home; songs be in every mouth; lo, from the north we come, from east, and west, and south. City of God, the bond are free, we come to live and reign in thee!

CHARLES E. OAKLEY (1832–65)

CATHERINE B

Holy Spirit: the Pentecost promise

'I will show wonders in the heaven above and signs on the earth below… before the coming of the great and glorious day of the Lord. And everyone who calls on the name of the Lord will be saved.'

The disciples were accused of being drunk—but they were intoxicated with the Holy Spirit, not wine. The Holy Spirit, so often depicted as a gentle dove, is here a flame that sets hearts on fire, to the extent that disciples who had cowered in fear for their lives as Jesus was crucified are now boldly preaching to crowds in the city streets. The fire didn't go out and they, like millions of Jesus' followers since then, were martyred for their faith.

As we come to the end of the year, and to the end of this series on the hope we have in Christ, ask God for new boldness to share your faith with others in the coming year. Ask him for eyes to see what he is doing in the lives of people around you, so that you can pray specifically for their needs, speaking up when that's appropriate. Ask for Jesus' servant-heart to love the unlovely people you meet. Ask for hands that reach out in love and blessing to others, and feet that go the extra mile into difficult places and situations to bring God's peace.

Ask for fresh hope to see God's transforming power at work in the situations you pray for, which have seemed beyond hope. Look back over the past two weeks and let your faith be strengthened by the stories of God's intervention in the lives of so many who hoped when all hope had gone.

Have a hope-filled New Year!

....

And our eyes at last shall see him, through his own redeeming love, for that Child so dear and gentle is our Lord in heav'n above, and he leads his children on to the place where he is gone.

Cecil Frances Humphreys Alexander (1818–95)

CATHERINE B

Other Christina Press titles

Who'd Plant a Church? Diana Archer (£5.99)
Planting an Anglican church from scratch, with a team of four—two adults and two children—is an unusual adventure even in these days. Diana Archer gives a distinctive perspective on parish life.

Pathway Through Grief edited by Jean Watson (£6.99)
Ten Christians, each bereaved, share their experience of loss. Frank and sensitive accounts offering comfort and reassurance to those recently bereaved and new insights to those involved in counselling.

God's Catalyst Rosemary Green (£8.99)
Insight, inspiration and advice for both counsellors and concerned Christians who long to be channels of God's Spirit to help those in need. A unique tool for the non-specialist counsellor.

Angels Keep Watch Carol Hathorne (£5.99)
After 40 years, Carol Hathorne obeyed God's call to Kenya. She came face to face with dangers, hardships and poverty, but experienced the joy of learning that Christianity is still growing in God's world.

Not a Super-Saint Liz Hansford (£6.99)
Describes the outlandish situations that arise in the Manse, where life is both fraught and tremendous fun. A book for the ordinary Christian who feels they must be the only one who hasn't quite got it together.

The Addiction of a Busy Life Edward England (£5.99)
Twelve lessons from a devastating heart attack. Edward, a giant of Christian publishing in the UK, and founder of Christina Press, shares what the Lord taught him when his life nearly came to an abrupt end.

Life Path Luci Shaw (£5.99)
Keeping a journal can enrich life as we live it, and bring it all back later. Luci Shaw shows how a journal can also help us grow in our walk with God.

Precious to God Sarah Bowen (£5.99)
Two young people have their expectations shattered by the birth of a handicapped child. What was initially a tragedy is, through faith, transformed into a story of inspiration, hope and spiritual enrichment.

Other BRF titles

The Incredible Journey Steve Brady (£7.99)
The Bible presents the ultimate adventure—God's incredible, personal journey to the human race, which he loves with an amazing love, despite its repeated rejection of him. The story culminates in the coming of Jesus Christ, the incarnate God, in the events we celebrate every Christmas. This book of readings for Advent and Christmas shows how Jesus has come to take us home to God, no matter what our starting point. When we embark on the road of life with him, we discover that we never walk alone.

Shaping the Heart Pamela Evans (£6.99)
God created the human heart to be a worship-filled, holy place with himself in residence, a garden in which the fruit of the Spirit may grow. *Shaping the Heart* is a book for every Christian who wants their heart to become—through the healing and redemptive touch of heavenly grace and mercy—a place where God delights to dwell. *Shaping the Heart* is designed for practical use, whether as individual reading for a retreat or quiet day or for shared study and discussion in a group setting.

Story Box Bible Tales Eve Lockett (£8.99)
Story Box Bible Tales uses simple everyday objects and a variety of helpful prompts to encourage children to tell and share stories from the Bible, and interweave these stories with their experience of everyday life. All the stories are linked to key moments in life such as special times of year and significant milestones, or everyday themes such as holidays or making friends. The ideas provide an ideal opportunity for families to explore the Bible together at home and talk about the memories and activities they share.

Quiet Spaces: A light for my path Ed. Heather Fenton (£4.99)
'A light for my path' is how the psalmist described the word of God (Psalm 119:105). This theme is particularly important as we celebrate the 400th anniversary of the publication of the King James Version. The contributions for this edition of Quiet Spaces include Jean Watson on Saul's conversion, Carol Jerman ('A lamp to my feet'), Janet Fletcher ('The inner light of hope') and Alison McTier on 'Companions along the way', plus regular features from Tony Horsfall and Margaret Harvey.

You can order the titles on these two pages from Christina Press or BRF, using the order forms on pages 140 and 141.

Christina Press Publications Order Form

All of these publications are available from Christian bookshops everywhere or, in case of difficulty, direct from the publisher. Please make your selection below, complete the payment details and send your order with payment as appropriate to:

Christina Press Ltd, 17 Church Road, Tunbridge Wells, Kent TN1 1LG

		Qty	Price	Total
8700	God's Catalyst	____	£8.99	____
8701	Women Celebrating Faith	____	£5.99	____
8702	Precious to God	____	£5.99	____
8703	Angels Keep Watch	____	£5.99	____
8704	Life Path	____	£5.99	____
8705	Pathway Through Grief	____	£6.99	____
8706	Who'd Plant a Church?	____	£5.99	____
8707	Dear God, It's Me and It's Urgent	____	£6.99	____
8708	Not a Super-Saint	____	£6.99	____
8709	The Addiction of a Busy Life	____	£5.99	____
8710	In His Time	____	£5.99	____

POSTAGE AND PACKING CHARGES				
	UK	Europe	Surface	Air Mail
£7.00 & under	£1.25	£3.00	£3.50	£5.50
£7.01–£29.99	£2.25	£5.50	£6.50	£10.00
£30.00 & over	free	prices on request		

Total cost of books £ ____
Postage and Packing £ ____
TOTAL £ ____

All prices are correct at time of going to press, are subject to the prevailing rate of VAT and may be subject to change without prior warning.

Name _____

Address _____

_____

_____ Postcode _____

Total enclosed £ _____ (cheques should be made payable to 'Christina Press Ltd')

❏ Please do not send me further information about Christina Press publications

DBDWG0311

BRF Publications Order Form

All of these publications are available from Christian bookshops everywhere, or in case of difficulty direct from the publisher. Please make your selection below, complete the payment details and send your order with payment as appropriate to:

BRF, 15 The Chambers, Vineyard, Abingdon OX14 3FE

		Qty	Price	Total
003 5	The Incredible Journey	____	£7.99	____
726 6	Shaping the Heart	____	£6.99	____
810 2	Story Box Bible Tales	____	£8.99	____
661 0	Quiet Spaces: Tomorrow	____	£4.99	____
830 0	Quiet Spaces: Bread	____	£4.99	____
831 7	Quiet Spaces: Light	____	£4.99	____

POSTAGE AND PACKING CHARGES				
	UK	Europe	Surface	Air Mail
£7.00 & under	£1.25	£3.00	£3.50	£5.50
£7.01–£29.99	£2.25	£5.50	£6.50	£10.00
£30.00 & over	free	prices on request		

Total cost of books £ ____
Postage and Packing £ ____
TOTAL £ ____

All prices are correct at time of going to press, are subject to the prevailing rate of VAT and may be subject to change without prior warning.

Name _____

Address _____

_____ Postcode _____

Phone _____ Email _____

Total enclosed £ _____ (cheques should be made payable to 'BRF')

Please charge my Visa ❏ Mastercard ❏ Switch card ❏ with £ _____

Card no. ⬚⬚⬚⬚⬚⬚⬚⬚⬚⬚⬚⬚⬚⬚⬚⬚⬚⬚

Expires ⬚⬚⬚⬚   Security code ⬚⬚⬚

Issue no (Switch) ⬚⬚⬚⬚

Signature _____
(essential if paying by credit/Switch card)

❏ Please do not send me further information about BRF publications

Visit the BRF website at www.brf.org.uk

DBDWG0311

BRF is a Registered Charity

Subscription Information

Each issue of *Day by Day with God* is available from Christian bookshops everywhere. Copies may also be available through your church Book Agent or from the person who distributes Bible reading notes in your church.

Alternatively you may obtain *Day by Day with God* on subscription direct from the publishers. There are two kinds of subscription:

Individual Subscriptions are for four copies or less, and include postage and packing. To order an annual Individual Subscription, please complete the details on page 144 and send the coupon with payment to BRF in Abingdon. You can also use the form to order a Gift Subscription for a friend.

Church Subscriptions are for five copies or more, sent to one address, and are supplied post free. Church Subscriptions run from 1 May to 30 April each year and are invoiced annually. To order a Church Subscription, please complete the details opposite and send the coupon to BRF in Abingdon. You will receive an invoice with the first issue of notes.

All subscription enquiries should be directed to:

BRF
15 The Chambers
Vineyard
Abingdon
OX14 3FE

Tel: 01865 319700
Fax: 01865 319701
E-mail: subscriptions@brf.org.uk

Church Subscriptions

The Church Subscription rate for *Day by Day with God* will be £12.15 per person until April 2012.

❏ I would like to take out a church subscription for _____ (Qty) copies.

❏ Please start my order with the January 2012 / May 2012 / September 2012* issue. I would like to pay annually/receive an invoice with each edition of the notes*.
(*Please delete as appropriate)

Please do not send any money with your order. Send your order to BRF and we will send you an invoice. The Church Subscription year is from May to April. If you start subscribing in the middle of a subscription year we will invoice you for the remaining number of issues left in that year.

Name and address of the person organising the Church Subscription:

Name _____

Address _____

_____

_____

Postcode _____ Telephone _____
Church _____
Name of Minister _____

Name and address of the person paying the invoice if the invoice needs to be sent directly to them:

Name _____

Address _____

_____

Postcode _____ Telephone _____

Please send your coupon to:

BRF
15 The Chambers
Vineyard
Abingdon
Oxon
OX14 3FE

❏ Please do not send me further information about BRF publications

DBDWG0311   BRF is a Registered Charity

Individual Subscriptions

❏ I would like to give a gift subscription (please complete both name and address sections below)
❏ I would like to take out a subscription myself (complete your name and address details only once)

Your name _____

Your address _____

_____ Postcode _____

Tel _____ Email _____

Gift subscription name _____

Gift subscription address _____

_____ Postcode _____

Gift message (20 words max) _____

_____

Please send *Day by Day with God* for one year, beginning with the January 2012 / May 2012 / September 2012 issue: (delete as applicable)

	UK	Surface	Air Mail
Day by Day with God	❏ £15.15	❏ £17.25	❏ £20.25
2-year subscription	❏ £27.00	N/A	N/A

Please complete the payment details below and send your coupon, with appropriate payment, to BRF, 15 The Chambers, Vineyard, Abingdon, Oxon OX14 3FE

Total enclosed £ _____ (cheques should be made payable to 'BRF')
Please charge my Visa ❏ Mastercard ❏ Switch card ❏ with £ _____

Card no. ☐☐☐☐☐☐☐☐☐☐☐☐☐☐☐☐☐☐☐

Expires ☐☐☐☐ Security code ☐☐☐

Issue no (Switch) ☐☐☐☐

Signature _____
(essential if paying by credit/Switch card)

NB: These notes are also available from Christian bookshops everywhere.

❏ Please do not send me further information about BRF publications

DBDWG0311   BRF is a Registered Charity